East German Girl

ESCAPE FROM EAST TO WEST

East German Girl

ESCAPE FROM EAST TO WEST

Sigrid Jackson
and
Jacqualynn Bogle

iUniverse, Inc.
Bloomington

East German Girl
Escape from East to West

iUniverse books may be ordered through booksellers or by contacting:

iUniverse
1663 Liberty Drive
Bloomington, IN 47403
www.iuniverse.com
1-800-Authors (1-800-288-4677)

Because of the dynamic nature of the Internet, any web addresses or links contained in this book may have changed since publication and may no longer be valid. The views expressed in this work are solely those of the author and do not necessarily reflect the views of the publisher, and the publisher hereby disclaims any responsibility for them.

Any people depicted in stock imagery provided by Thinkstock are models, and such images are being used for illustrative purposes only.
Certain stock imagery © Thinkstock.

ISBN: 978-1-4620-4132-9 (sc)
ISBN: 978-1-4620-4133-6 (hc)
ISBN: 978-1-4620-4256-2 (ebk)

Library of Congress Control Number: 2011912851

Printed in the United States of America

iUniverse rev. date: 08//23/2011

Dedication

To my Mother, Johanna Kühl. In my heart and mind she is the main character in this book. Despite her human weaknesses and failures, she persevered and made it possible for me to be a free person.

ACKNOWLEDGEMENT:

- I need to acknowledge all of the people who crossed my path within the past 30 years and suggested that I should write a book after they heard about my life experiences. It set a spark in my heart and I started praying for the right time...well it took this long!

- A very special thanks to my talented, gifted granddaughter, Jacqualynn Bogle. Jacqualynn spent numerous hours during the past year writing, revising, and polishing my story. The book would not be what it is today without her involvement.

- Thank you Dr. Szopinski for deciphering my first rough manuscript, giving it the first light editing, and for your research of the war history.

- Thank you Dr. Reck for editing the finished manuscript. It was God that brought you back into our lives again at this special time.

- A great thank you to my family who put up with my ups and downs during this process for the past year. You all kept encouraging me and showed your faith and ability that I am able to fulfill my work, this book.

HOME

1941

I will sing and make music.

I, Sigrid Kühl, am a young girl with wispy, blonde curls and a captivating smile (or so I am told). My aunt Charlotte, who lives in the room on the upper level of our house, is constantly doting on me with such flattering, descriptive lines. I am thankful for her and that she has never married or had children because she lives with us and showers me with every toy imaginable.

Tante Charlotte and me.

At every chance, I pitter-patter up to her room and spend time with her sweetness. She tells me stories, and I especially love the stories about me. Charlotte loves children, but as I said, she never had any of her own. She begged and begged my parents to have another child, and so I was born. I guess that is the reason I was born seven years after Jörg. I think of her as my second mother.

My father's father also lives with us, and my mother and Charlotte take good care of him. I'm not sure if it's just because he is old or if there is something wrong with him, but Opa Kühl sure does walk awful slowly with his cane. I love that he lives with us, for he is so sweet, gentle and kind. He takes a daily walk, and I regularly accompany him. As we hold hands and stroll along the sidewalk, I am careful to look out for pebbles, sticks, or anything that might cause Opa Kühl to stumble or wobble on his cane, and similarly he looks out for me. Midway through our walk, we take a rest on a bench, and I am able to have all of my curiosity satisfied as Opa Kühl patiently answers my thousands of questions about life.

Opa Kühl and me on one of our strolls.

Thankfully, my father, Erich, has a highly respected job in the courts, so we are able to accommodate Charlotte and Opa Kühl in our house, which has all the modern conveniences. I am not able to appreciate the "greatness" others see in my father. I find myself mesmerized when he reads a book with opera playing in the background and his brow lines tell me that he is getting deep into the text. I am amazed when he plays an instrument, paints and draws, or whenever I overhear one of his poems. All of his talents fit perfectly with his tall stature, radiant blue eyes, and rich, dark hair. But, something tells me I don't mean much to him, or maybe he just told me that . . .

My father and me.

However, I do have Charlotte and Johanna, my gentle mother, for reassurance. Mother, although rather quiet, is very funny in nature and has a saying for everything. Mother is seven years older than my father;

however, she never seems older. In the times when I need it most, she comforts me the best she can, for she is not a demonstrative person. She pushes her board-straight dark brown hair away from her face and bends the small distance she has to until our matching, bluish-gray eyes meet, and through her eyes, I see strength and everything seems okay again.

My brother, Jörg, me, and my mother.

STETTIN GERMANY

1942

War will continue until the end.

Tension in the air thickens as sirens resound through the falling and inevitable booming of bombs manically uniting with the earth's floor. Canned foods that line the cold, concrete walls rattle as the earth shakes from the commotion such an uninvited union has caused. The dark blanket of night reaches down to flood our little cellar, packed with my family and neighbors who join our shelter and help to console one another. In times like this, there are no strangers, only enemies, and we know those are the growling jets flying overhead.

Only silence exists within our four walls. Any other noise we hear is just outside pollution. But, this is not a serene silence. Too much uncertainty weighs down upon the room. Questions dart through our minds, "Will the next bomb land on our homes?" "Are there enemy soldiers entering our houses as we helplessly take cover?" As we endure the night, a minuscule thread of security is present because we know that we are well-equipped with blankets and food to last us several days.

The silence in our cellar is interrupted by a sudden power surge. The radio flicks on, and a powerful, deep, confident voice informs us, the cowering citizens of a tiny town, of the enemy's position and other updates that are too complicated for me, a four year old, to comprehend. This voice makes us feel connected with the events that are playing out above. For those of us who say the glass is half empty, play-by-play images form in our minds; some, perhaps, are horribly exaggerated. Possibly, from that voice, false hope is instilled in those of us who believe that the glass is half full. This is just another night that blindly drags on and pulls at all our human emotions. My brother, Jörg, sits next to me, and I can feel the weight of his worry.

Because of this ongoing war, spending the night in the cellar is quite a frequent event for us and it is certainly frightening, but the anxiety has become too much for me. The nights have become long and boring with no one willing to talk, and being young, I need something to occupy my mind. I decide to practice my whistle. I moisten my lips with my tongue and inhale deeply and blow through the tunnel I have created. A faint sound escapes, but I know that even with all of my practice, I have not yet mastered the whistle.

My father is an extremely talented, handsome man. He creates life-like paintings and drawings, writes captivating poetry, and plays several instruments with finesse. Jörg is beginning to become very good at these things too, and they connect in these areas. Unfortunately, that connection doesn't include me. I yearn to learn an instrument, and I have decided to start with the harmonica. Before my father left for the war, I asked him to teach me and begged my brother to help me, but they both just laughed. I concluded that I would just teach myself to play the harmonica, just like I taught myself to whistle.

With all these countless nights in the cellar, I have defeated the uncomfortable silence with the notes of my harmonica. With all the practice, my skill has drastically improved, and I feel a great deal of pride in my accomplishment.

I know what waits for us on mornings after being in the cellar. Jörg and I will run up the hill near our house to overlook the city of Stettin'[1] where our mother's parents live. As every time before, I know the sight of the aftermath will be devastating and make my heart sink. Just like a replayed horror scene, the distant flames will be shooting high and the trailing smoke will cause my mother to panic about her parents' safety. I am haunted by these awful wartime routines.

---

[1]   Stettin, Germany was captured by the Soviet Red Army April 26, 1945. The city was officially turned over to Poland July 5, 1945. The city is now named Szczecin.

A DIVIDED GERMANY

(BACKGROUND)

Watch out for those who cause division.

Yes, I was young, but war-memories do not have an age requirement. War forces you to mature and gives you no choice but to cope with the realities of the world. Here we were, hiding for our lives and earnestly listening to the government, who, unbeknownst to us, was feeding us lies.

The political aftermath of WWII resulted in an incoming communistic government and a divided Germany. Soon, the division would be official and by 1949, there would be an East and a West Germany. Countries from the Eastern part of Europe were moving into Germany during her vulnerable time, and at the conclusion of the war chaos I would live through, my home, Germany, would be segregated from the West and I would become part of the East (Deutsche Demokratische Republik).

Soon thereafter, I would hear continual messages about Stalin, the beloved idol and ruler of Russia. His chiseled face was plastered everywhere. His statue was larger than life and mounted in public places for all people to see and to be intimidated by it. Lenin would be worshiped as the Father of Communism, a relic from World War I. Foreign soldiers would march in our streets and live among us, just as if they owned our country. I guess they did.

When the Soviets took charge, freedom was a thing of the past. We were there only to work and obey. We were expected and forced by fear to keep our mouths closed. See nothing. Hear nothing. We were to do only as commanded. Laws were signed without any input from taxpaying citizens, and complaints were forbidden. Even in our schools, we had to take a class of the Russian language to further assimilate us. Communism would discard God and the Bible. The "leaders" were the gods, and, to them, God and church were just a crutch for weak people. The punishment for speaking against the "government gods" was harsh and long, often an inhumane labor camp.

It is a very dark world when the government takes over little by little sneakily and fools its citizens. The sales pitch for communism was catchy, but the product was not. Conditions of every realm were poor.

Hospitals would become primitive and lack modern equipment, for there would be no money left for such luxuries, as everything would be "free" and paid by the government. Food supplies would be meager. For just a small bag of potatoes, we would have to stand in line for hours. An announcement would be made each day when all of the food items were out, so all of the people who were still in line would go home without anything to fill their empty bellies, including my family. Then, we would have to repeat the same scenario the next day in the hopes that this time we would be lucky and receive whatever we had stayed in line for all day and the day before so that we could have some nourishment.

Such deprivation led to people stooping so low as to turn in friends for a piece of bread, clothes on their back, or a warm place to stay. At that time in our family's cellar, huddling among our comforting neighbors, we did not foresee that before long we would have to watch our every move and every person because no one, not even our best of friends, could be trusted.

NO MORE DAILY STROLLS

But there is a friend who sticks closer
than a brother.

After a long night of bombing, Opa Kühl didn't show up for our walk. So I thought to myself, *"Okay, he is sick today."*

But today he didn't show up again, so I better ask Mother what's wrong.

"Where is Opa?"

"Well, Siddi," that's what my mom always calls me, "his heart was very weak and he has passed away."

"I want to see him, Mom."

"He's lying in the washroom, dear."

I really do want to see my loving Opa, so to the washroom I go.

As I step into the washroom, the air hits me like a stiff board. Something isn't right because anywhere Opa is, the mood is always happy. Instead he's just laying there so still as if he is sleeping. I better tell him how I feel like I always do on our walks.

"I miss you so much, Opa. I love you, and I know you are in heaven now just like you told me we would all go there some day."

"Siddi?"

Apparently Mother had sneaked around the corner. I wonder how much she heard.

"The mortuary people will pick Opa Kühl up, but it won't be for a couple of days because they are busy taking care of the war victims."

Again, I look at him. I will miss Opa very much, but I don't want to come back in here in the next couple of days until they come and take him away. This is my last time seeing my walking buddy.

AMBIVALENT REUNION

SUMMER 1943

From the lips of children
comes praise and truth.

Mother, Jörg, and me at our home in Stettin.

During all of this bombing, screaming sirens, and running in and out of shelters, the children around our area became ill with an extremely contagious disease, diphtheria. We were stowed away in hospitals under quarantine. The diphtheria spread rapidly, and I was stuck in a depressing, crowded hospital. With the seemingly endless boredom and loneliness, my fears of never leaving this brighter version of a bunker mounted.

Dazed and dulled by my illness as usual, I lay in my hospital bed gazing above at the yellowed, cracking ceiling. My zone of ringing silence was interrupted when the nurse came over to my side and without explanation, assisted me out of bed and led me to the waiting room. As I entered the room, everything seemed normal. The room was still sectioned off by a huge glass window to protect the outside, older world from us.

The nurse tugged at my hand a little to get my attention, so I looked at her. With squinted eyes and a calm voice she informed me, "There is someone out there who very much wants to see you."

She then gestured her hand toward the big glass window, so once again, I shifted my eyes. A soldier stood on the other side of the transparent wall, and he was looking at me and smiling. I was afraid of him and started to cry. He was dressed in a German infantry soldier uniform, including those horrible, shiny, scary looking boots. I was horrified of the boots that all soldiers had to wear. They brought images to my mind of crusading soldiers marching through the streets and then the stamping of their feet together to greet an officer. Shuffle. Stomp! Shuffle. Stomp! Scuff. Dreadful noises!

Finally, I built up the courage to look into this man's eyes, and, even through the glare on the glass, I could see tears streaming down his face while he kept mouthing, "Ich bin dein Pappi."[2] Through his weather-worn skin and stress-filled eyes, I began to see the identity of this man. To me, his words were empty. He was practically a stranger. The word "Pappi" did not overjoy me. It's hard to feel emotions for someone whom you had seen so little of, even when he was home (a long time ago). My legs started to shake and my body grew weak from a combination of nerves and diphtheria. I no longer felt like standing there, so I turned around and went back to my bed.

But, today, Jörg came by to talk to me and he confirmed that the man who had been behind the glass was our father. Jörg scolded me and said that I should have been nicer because our father would be back in Poland and Russia under the orders of our country by the time I got back home. Maybe Jörg was right, but again, I felt little emotion about the situation.

---

2 "I am your Daddy."

CHANGE KNOCKING
AT OUR DOOR

God is our refuge and strength.

This morning an event occurred for which there was no way we could have been prepared.

We were awakened by penetrating pounds at our front door. Alarmed, Mother scurried to answer while I sprang out of bed to view it all from around the corner. A daunting figure of a soldier in uniform with those awful boots stood in our door shouting orders.

"*Leave* . . ."

Mother's face drained of all color.

"*Relocate* . . ."

Her eyes became glazed.

"*Immediately* . . ."

Her hands started trembling.

"*or else* . . ."

Her chest heaved as reality sunk in. Mother gave a prompt nod as the soldier turned and left. Shuffle. Stomp!

Her reaction combined with the aftershock of the soldier's harsh voice caused my head to spin. I couldn't make sense of it. No longer hiding, I hurry to my mother, but she is in a state of shock and can't console herself, let alone me.

"Mother," I'm trying to speak to her like her brave girl, "what did that soldier say?"

Her eyes roam the room, flit past my gaze, and focus on the window.

"The soldier was here to protect us."

She swallows hard. I don't think those words taste good to her.

"The enemy plans to target our town, so it is no longer safe here." Now she looks at me, "Quickly, go pack only one suitcase with what you really need. Hurry now! I'll wake Jörg and Charlotte."

Where are we going? When will we come back home? I dare not ask Mother now, but how can this be happening so quickly? Maybe it will be like the bomb shelters and we will return home in a few days.

RELOCATION

(1944)

There is a place prepared for us.

Goodness! I have never seen so many people rushing around the train station like this. I recognize some of the children from the hospital, trailing behind their mothers. They look much healthier now.

"This way, Sigrid!"

Mom keeps tugging at my hand, almost yanking my doll to the ground, and she is walking so briskly through the station. I feel like a train car with Mother pulling me and, Jörg, close behind me seems like a caboose.

I break free of my mother's hand because I see Charlotte heading towards us. I push through the crowd until I can finally wrap my arms around her leg.

"We're going this way," I inform her.

But, Charlotte just replies, "I know, darling. I have to go this way. Your mother and I are just following orders and that means I have to go this way."

No! No! Something tells me now that we'll be gone longer than a couple days.

"Don't worry." She is just saying this because she can see my troubled thoughts all over my face. "I will see you soon, and when I do, I'll have a new toy for you." Her grin is contagious and I can no longer resist it, so I smile.

"Aufwiedersehen meine Liebe!"

She was gone.

"Goodbye, my love!"

"Sigrid! You must stick with me!" Mother calls, so I quickly rejoin her.

TRAIN RIDE INTO THE UNKNOWN

Peace I leave with you; My peace I give you.

Our train pulls up, and we continue through the station. Finally, we come to a screeching halt. We have reached our platform but we must make our way through the mass of mothers and children, which keeps mounting like sand in an hourglass. Suitcases pound me from behind while waistcoats brush my legs in front. Above all of the clicking feet on the chilled concrete, I can hear a soldier's voice cracking out orders. Everyone is inching toward him like lost puppies. It is obvious that Mother doesn't know exactly where we are headed. For now, we are just worried about getting to our train car.

The frigid air is beginning to bite at my face and I can feel it filtering through my coat. My doll has practically frozen. I bet that Jörg's teddy bear must be close to freezing also.

I want to know what is going on, but jumping up to look over the crowd to see would not do me any good, and the crowd is too thick to see through. However, by getting close to the ground, there are tiny peepholes around all the shoes. The tracks are empty, so I guess we are waiting for the train to arrive. Suddenly, the overhead speakers turn on, and crackling static pours out from them.

"Attention! Everyone, get down on the ground! American planes are headed our way! I repeat everyone on the ground!"

Now a panic overtakes the crowd of terrified people who start screaming. Mothers are pulling their children to the ground, but at least the sprawled bodies create a little heat with which to combat the freezing floor. Our intermingled bodies all hush in unison. I desperately wish I was in our cellar back home!

The sky is growling at us. One plane passes, then another and another.

"Mother, I'm scared," I don't think she can hear me, so I tap on her hand which is over my shoulder and repeat, "Mother, I'm scared."

This only makes her wrap her arm further around me and cover my mouth with her hand. She looks so calm, even though the sky is angry, and she still doesn't know where we're going. I know I have to be strong too.

The sky is calming down now and people are begging to untangle themselves so they can get to their feet. The crowd continues to shuffle onward as Mother, Jörg, and I enter the funnel the people are sifting through as they head toward the soldier who is barking out orders. Finally, we reach him and his surrounding entourage, which I had not seen when I was at the back of the crowd.

"Dein Name?"[3]

One of the soldier's entourage just aggressively stepped out to us like a dog approaching fresh meat.

"Johanna Kühl," answers Mother as two other members of the entourage look over his shoulder as he skims a secret list.

"Um hum."

His finger lands somewhere on the mysterious list. The two others nod firmly and robotically shove us a short distance in the right direction as the locomotive moves through the station and pulls up alongside us. We file into our train car along with the rest of the war victims, and together we head into the unknown.

---

3   "Your name?"

IN THE UNKNOWN, ANKLAM

For the world is Mine and all that is in it.

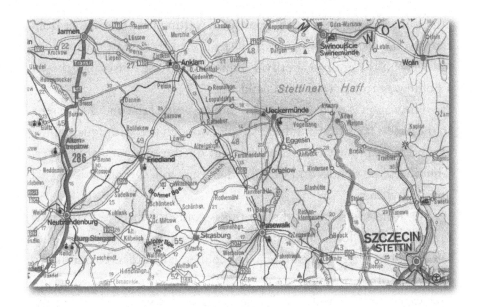

After a long and cramped train ride filled with mothers soothing their crying babies, it feels good to land my feet on stable ground. Signs are everywhere that read, "Anklam" or, "Welcome to Anklam". So, apparently Anklam is our destination. Once again, Mother, Jörg and I line up to follow a soldier who is waiting on the platform for us. As before, Mother briskly leads the way.

It seems as if everything around me is racing by as I slowly press on. I cannot understand what is happening because of my dazed state. Everything is so surreal, and the only reality is that I am far from home. Normally, I would be running up to Charlotte about this time of day, and she would be waiting for my daily visit, happily prepared to embrace me. How I wish she could embrace me right now! Somehow she would be able to slow down all of these scary changes that are happening. How I long for her warm embrace, but she is "far away" as Mother says and I don't even know where "far away" is.

Just the thought of Charlotte seems to bring me out of my daze enough to realize that we have stopped walking. The soldier is telling us what's about to happen, but I cannot process it (or maybe I have learned to tune soldiers out). One thing that keeps catching my attention, though, is an earthy, ripe smell wafting toward my nose from the two horses and a wagon that just pulled up. Based on what they have left on the ground already, I didn't think those horses had chosen a polite way to welcome us to Anklam.

The wagon is rickety and worn, unlike some of the ones I have seen in the streets back home. It has a simple, wooden bed with squat railing around it to protect the people who sit on the two parallel benches. The wheels are slender and wobbly when they roll. Overall, it is rugged and uninviting.

Regardless, it seems as though this is going to wheel us to our new home. Mother, Jörg, and I pile into the wagon following two other families of mothers and children. The soldier gives orders to our driver, and we're off. Crumbled pieces of earth dance around the wheels of our wagon to the steady rhythm of the horses' hooves. No one in the wagon dares disrupt this party going on in celebration of our highly anticipated destination of . . . . refuge.

Everyone sits completely helpless and lost because all we want is to rest our weary bodies. I know that I am far away from the awful, heart wrenching noise of sirens warning us that another attack from the sky is possible and to take shelter. No longer will I hear the echo of bombs flying through the air followed by the blinding explosions and then the sky ablaze with fires.

Finally, my mind has found rest in the quietness around me, hearing only the snorting of the horses and their trotting on the dusty sandy roads. I ponder about what the next day will hold. How will it be after I awake in the morning? What will face us? Can I play, sing, or ever laugh again?

ARRIVING ON THE FARM

All things become new. The old is gone.

Here we are at our destination, a huge farmhouse outside a tiny town called Tramstow. Mother says that it's so small she's never even heard of it, but she does know we are far from home.

"Fine with me, Mom," I assure her. "Just as long as I can sleep with you and my doll by my side, I am happy."

What is the smell here? The aroma in the air is something I have never inhaled before, but it is such a concoction that I cannot put my finger on just what it is I smell.

"Farm animals," Mother informs me.

So farm animals I guess it is, but I know that can't be the only thing because every once in awhile, when the breeze grazes my nose just right, I get a whiff of a sweet, fresh fragrance. I suppose it's nature abundant with trees, swaying grass, and fertile earth. This freshness is so new to me, and I much rather prefer it over the smell of smoke and burnt materials drifting through the air.

With all of this newness to take in, I just miss Aunt Charlotte and I hope she is safe, too, or even happy . . . . I wonder if she misses me. I have so many questions, but my exhaustion is overpowering my curiosity, and I just want to go to lie down.

As we pull up to the house in our rickety wagon, I can see the farmer's family waiting outside to greet us. One by one, Mother, Jörg, and I step down from the wagon, and to my surprise, so does everybody else who was in the wagon. Two other families are also going to be staying here, I guess, but I'm glad they have some kids my age I can play with.

"Welcome!"

The farmer's daughter, Elfriede, greets us along with her two sons and her mother, the farmer's wife. I bet the farmer is away at war like my dad is. Regardless, they seem so warm and I can't believe they are so happy about all of us staying at their house. I know nobody had a choice here, but it is such a relief to be welcomed by these kind people.

Right to business, Elfriede takes us to our rooms. She guides us through a very large country kitchen with two cooking stoves on each side.

"Your room is right off the kitchen," Elfriede tells Mother as she opens the door.

There are two single beds separated by a small night stand. On the other side of the room is a couch with a coffee table.

"This table will be where you eat," Elfriede explains to Mother.

She shows us a chest of drawers to share for our clothing. Mother murmurs to hush Jörg's expression assuring that it is plenty of space for our few belongings. Elfriede opens another door right by our little seating area that leads to a roomy walk-in pantry.

"Mother, are you happy?" I ask.

"There is room for our groceries and lots of storage space to organize," she responds with a half-grin.

Elfriede kindly interrupts our little conversation and proceeds to give Mother more information and instructions regarding the kitchen facilities and rules.

"You will cook on the large stove, Frau Kühl," instructs Elfriede, and she rolls out more rules to Mother like the time of the day that she can cook and how much time she will have to use the stove. Elfriede explains that all four families share the kitchen, and each family is to use their own cooking items.

"You have a good night now," she utters, holding the door handle in her hand to leave our room.

"Good night, Elfriede," Mother replies, "Thank you for giving us a shelter. It was not my decision to intrude. Sorry the government took away your privacy and part of your property by having to take in three strange families."

Elfriede turns around and with a smile on her face and with a gentle voice she replies, "The Lord will take care of us all."

Mother looks at my brother and me, and all we can do is hug and cry as the door closes.

LIFE ON THE FARM

(1946)

He who gathers crops in the summer
is a wise person.

I feel so grateful that God has put us on this enormous farm with Elfriede and her family, but things have not been all roses. Even though the war is over, the soldiers are still gone and nothing is normal. My mom and the mothers of the other two families were informed that they now have to work in the fields in exchange for the food we are getting.

I remember Mother telling Jörg and me that she was a secretary and made her own living working in an office before she and my father got married. She told us about how she had to study to be successful and master old German handwriting, which I have heard is very difficult. When I've tried to peer over Mother's shoulder before when she's reading, I couldn't understand a word of it. It's almost like a different language. And when Mother sees my eyes grow really big in awe of this strange language, she just laughs and says, "You should try to decipher my shorthand, Siddi."

I knew when Elfriede told her that she would have to be a field hand that it was going to be tough compared to the work she's used to. Mother is good at reading and writing, but I don't think I've ever seen her do hard labor before.

So Mother has been out in the fields 8-10 hours everyday (except Sunday, of course). They have her planting some crops and harvesting others. This leaves me alone a lot of the time, and by the end of the day she is too tired to talk to me or do anything. So I have tried to follow Mother's advice and make new friends. This is kind of hard since all of the girls in the other families are teenagers and have to help in the fields, too.

Because of my loneliness, I finally built up the courage to go to the apartment downstairs one day. I had seen one of the boys from another family who had been running around the farm a lot lately and he seemed fun, so even though I was scared that he might not want to play with me, I am glad that I did because now that boy and I are best friends. My best friend's name is Wolfgang.

No longer am I lonely for 8-10 hours a day because Wolfgang and I *always* have fun with each other. It doesn't even matter that I am a girl and he's a boy or that I am two years older than him. We do the silliest things together, and sometimes I am afraid we'll get reprimanded.

Today we are going to get Harry, an older boy who lives upstairs, to come play with us. Just the other day we had all played hide-and-go-seek in the hay stalls, but today the plan is to mess around with the farm animals.

"Come on, Harry!"

Wolfgang is so impatient! He always yells like we are in a rush or something. Harry knows not to keep him waiting, and as he is coming towards us down the stairs, he nearly trips and falls on his face.

"Are you ready for some fun?" I ask Harry with a cheesy smile.

"Sure am," he replies. Harry doesn't say much.

So we make our way over to the pens where the animals are kept. I could walk with my eyes closed and know how close we are to the animals just based on the smell of manure and warm hay that is growing thick in the air.

Whoosh!

Wolfgang sprints past me, jumps up on the railing surrounding the animals, and lets out a hoot! Such a commotion causes the animals to scatter and fill the air with dust from their push-off from the earth.

"Your turn!" he yells to Harry and me, but we just look at each other and smile.

For a moment I think about how crazy Wolfgang is, but I love it.

Whoosh!

Dust particles are bombarding my eyes, and my braids are probably sticking straight out from the back of my head. Now it's my turn, so I let out a hoot!

The animals back further away from the rails, but unfortunately, the effect of my hoot is not as dramatic as Wolfgang's so I walk away defeated.

"How about this?"

Disappointed and embarrassed, I am glad Harry has already stolen the attention. He is on the other side of the pen where the pigs are now huddling and appears to be holding a long branch in his hand. Harry extends the branch between the rails and into the animals' dwelling. As he pushes it farther, the branch draws close to meeting the backside of a hefty sow.

Already the animals are shaken up, and their eyes are fixed on Wolfgang and me from across the pen. Harry's mischievous grin continues to spread across his face as he reaches his arm farther and farther, and now his shoulders are vertical to the rails and his body is stretched across the ground. I can see the tension surging through his limbs as he tries to make the last couple of centimeters, and all Wolfgang and I can do is watch in silence.

One centimeter . . . two . . . *squeal!*

Pigs are now dashing for me and Wolfgang, but they are like ghosts on a vengeance pushing through the thick cloud of dust. Afraid they might break through the pen, we climb into a nearby tree as squeals rise around us. I hope Mother doesn't hear them all the way out in the field.

The anger of the pigs reminds me of Hans, the farmer's grandson, and how he reacts when Wolfgang and I secretly steal his sandwich everyday. The only difference is that Hans doesn't know it is us, but I think the pigs know and they want to do something about it.

"Where's Harry?" I ask Wolfgang with great concern, but he just points to a brown figure rushing towards the tree. The brown figure heaves itself up into the refuge of the branches, and now I can see that it is a mud and dust-caked Harry.

"What is going on out here?!"

All of our faces drop, and our fear shifts from the pigs to the shrill voice calling out from the house. It is Frau Hannemann, the farmer's wife. She is a plain woman with a hard face and a biting voice. Even though I keep my distance from her, I have seen Frau Hannemann snap on some of the other kids, and I fear what's in store for us. Collectively,

Harry, Wolfgang, and I turn to each other and, as if we can read each other's minds, we know what to do.

Simultaneously, we spring out from the fork in the tree where we have been crouching and head in the exact opposite direction of the house. We are running so fast that my braids are probably going to be yanked off by the wind, but I would rather have no braids for the rest of my life than face the wrath of Frau Hannemann and the pigs.

SOLDIERS ON THE FARM

(1947)

When the enemy comes in like a flood,
He makes a way of escape.

"But let all who take refuge in you be glad; let them ever sing for joy. Spread your protection over them, that those who love your name may rejoice in you. Psalms 5:11."

Frau Hannemann's choice of scripture this Sunday is all too relevant. I think that God has put His protection over us by putting us with such good people. The music that flows from the fingers of Elfriede as she plays some hymns on the piano seems to be wrapping around us all packed here in this room. It's almost as if God is giving us a big hug and letting us know that no matter what, He will protect us.

Knock! Knock! Knock!

Everyone's face freezes. Someone is at the door. I stretch my body a little to see over the windowsill and through the recently washed glass. Through the haze that is covering the farm like a blanket, I can see who it is . . . soldiers.

My mind is racing and trying to think of what to do, but I can't seem to think past a wall of memories. We have had soldiers on the farm many times before, for they usually come needing a place to stay and waste no time taking over our rooms. At times it seems as though we are living at the end of the earth, secluded and far away from all of the noise and catastrophe of war, but it still manages to visit us. Polish, Czech, and Russian soldiers have all invaded our farm before, and we all know what to expect from each.

The Polish soldiers are very demanding. As soon as they arrive they demand food, and it has to be the finest we have. They go through our belongings and take whatever they please. Without hesitation they take over our rooms and expect them to be cleaned. I don't think they are capable of giving a kind expression or grateful word.

The stress we feel with the Polish doesn't even compare to the sheer terror that washes over us when the Czechs come. Mother hates them because she says they have caused me to grow up too quickly and know things I shouldn't know, even though I don't fully understand it all. When they arrive on the farm they don't go through our belongings and look for things to take like the Polish soldiers do. Instead they come looking for the women and girls. Some of the women have tried hiding their daughters, but that never works. They have their teenage daughters hide in the stalls and bury themselves under the hay, but these wild dogs scour the farm and dig and do what they have to do until they find their lost bones. Once they find all of the females, they make us sit on the floor in a straight line. The Czech soldiers remind me of the pigs on the farm. Their faces light up as they walk past us just like the pigs' faces do when I take food out to their pen. They're filthy creatures.

They make their picks. Any female who isn't too old or young and is without illness will do for these hogs. After they make their picks, I don't know where they go but the rest of us left in line can always hear screams of horror and agony mixed with wailings of sorrow and helplessness. And whenever the younger girls are chosen, the mothers just sit and sob as a soldier holds a machine gun to their heads.

One time, though, the women got creative when they had warning that another group of Czech soldiers was coming. Since they won't choose grandmas, very young children, or the sick, the women gave us all a disguise. I had to be a toddler, so Mother wrapped me up in a blanket, gave me a bottle to hold, and told me to suck my thumb. She dressed up like an old, frail lady. She covered her head with a shawl and shook all over as if she had some kind of disease. One woman acted as if she had a mental disorder. Every adult and child had a role to play, and we must have played the roles well because out of our group not one person was desirable enough for them to pick.

Also, we have had female Russian soldiers on the farm. Although their tactics are minor compared to the Czechs', they are still crude beings. They burst into our farmhouse, and without delay, they raid all of the women's drawers for clothes. Then they parade in front of us all dressed up in our mothers' clothes and laugh at us. I always try not to look at their faces because their eyes are a shallow pool only filled with hateful pleasure. How can they get so much joy from tormenting us?

"It's the Russians!"

In a flash, any trace of God and religion is tucked away. The Russians have been known to torture people who have Bibles or believe in God because the German Secret Service does not allow Bibles, so Mother tells me. Our experiences are less violent but still heartbreaking. We have had all of our Bibles thrown in a pile and set on fire. On another occasion, after digging our Bibles out of the garden where we had hidden them, they ripped every single page out in front of us, and then set them on fire.

"Is everything hidden?" Frau Hannemann asks in a panicked whisper.

We all just nod in reply, and she answers the door.

"Hello. Welcome." She greets them as kindly as she can despite her fears.

"Hello, ma'am. We would like some food."

He must be the officer of the other three soldiers lurking behind him. He seems nicer than the other Russian soldiers who have visited.

"Yes, sir. Come on in." Now she directs herself to all of our frozen faces, "Well, go on!"

We all scurry off. Some to clean up and others to prepare food. All I can think is something seems different. They can have all of the food they want as long as they don't hurt any of us, so with joy I help prepare the soldiers' meals.

VIKTER

If your enemy is hungry, give him food.

The soldiers have been here for a little over a week now, and they are definitely a nicer group than we are used to. Their officer is very strict. I have caught him reprimanding and even slapping the soldiers when they got out of line on several occasions, but I guess it keeps them polite.

I suppose they are here just to rest and get some nourishment (which I am sure they have considering they have nearly eaten us dry), but today they are leaving and jumping back out into the mess that we have been somewhat secluded from. Honestly, I am a little sad to see them go.

For the past week I have been a very nosey girl. Almost like their shadow, I would follow them around the farm and watch them from a distance. They amazed me. Here they intruded our farm and demanded several favors of us, yet they are kind and make me feel safe. I even watch them eat their dinner (after I have worked so hard to help prepare it). The officer and his three soldiers would all gather around the dining room table, adorned with a feast beyond what I have ever dreamt, and they would dig into it. It did satisfy me to see the looks on their faces with every bite. Looks of approval. But one of the soldier's faces gave me a look that was more loving than just plain old approval. The other three ignored the fact that I was shadowing their every move, but he would smile at me and acknowledge my presence. I had heard his officer call him Vikter.

After several days of me watching them longingly eat their feast, Vikter unglued his eyes from the wonderful food and looked at me in my corner of the room and asked, "Would you like to come eat with me?" as he motioned me toward the table.

I was not about to object because I was starving, so I just nodded and walked over to him. Immediately, he sat me on his lap and gave me control of the fork. I had the rights to any of the delicious foods that were spread across the table, and I took full advantage of it! Vikter just kind of chuckled as I stuffed fork-load after fork-load of food into my mouth, but I could see a slight look of annoyance from our other dinner guests. Regardless, this became the routine for the past couple of days, and he even demanded that I have my own plate.

Vikter, in just a short amount of time, has become like a father to me. My father has been away at war most of my life. He has never been proud of me anyway. And on the farm, there are no men here except for Wolfgang's dad, and he keeps to himself because he has a lot of seizures. Having Vikter care for me and give me hugs when I am sad is something new to me. He really thinks I am special, and I wish he would never leave.

It is inevitable though. Today the soldiers are leaving, and we are preparing to give them a nice send-off because they have been so kind to us. While the others have been preparing, I have been with Vikter and the soldiers. I helped him gather his things and we always talk (even though he is hard to understand). Now, as we make our way to the front of the farmhouse, hand-in-hand, my heart is running faster than Wolfgang escaping trouble. Elfriede and a couple of the other women are standing with goods in-hand to give to our kind, departing visitors.

"It was lovely having you and your men, officer," Elfriede steps forward to present the food we prepared for the soldiers for their journey.

"Thank you for your hospitality," the officer nods and accepts our gift.

One-by-one, the soldiers file into their jeep, Vikter is still holding my hand and I hope he doesn't let go. Vikter is the final soldier ready to hop into the jeep, but instead he turns around to face me. With no words, just a smile, he picks me up, sets me in the jeep, and then hops in.

The officer starts up the engine, and with a puff of smoke, we are off. He is driving slowly, but the jeep is still being jostled about on the uneven drive. No worries though because Vikter is holding me and I know that with him I am safe. I am glad that he is not leaving me. These past couple of days he has made me happy and been the father that I have never had, and Mother even knows that he is good to me and wants the best for me.

Swiveling my head around to the proper angle, I can see out of the narrow window in the back of the jeep. Even through the narrow window, the farmhouse looks smaller and smaller with every second. *What am I doing?*

A sudden slap of panic hits me like the officer slapping his soldiers into shape. I can't go with Vikter. Russia is so far away. I love him and I know he would be an excellent father to me, but what about Mother and Jörg? I would miss them too much, and I would break my mother's heart.

"Nooo! Siddi! My daughter! . . ."

Behind the jeep, following its trail, a steady stream of dust is being kicked up from the steps of a frantic person. I squint my eyes and peer through the narrow window, and emerging from the cloud is my mother!

"Vikter! My mother . . ." I tug at his sleeve and point behind us.

He looks back and sees what I have called to his attention, and slowly, he turns around with a stone face. Why is he not doing anything? I have to get off! Emotions are rushing out of me like blood from the slap that hit me earlier. I just look at Vikter with tears splashing from my eyes and into my lap, but there is nothing I can say.

"Stop!"

Vikter jerks on the shoulder of his officer and commands him to stop the vehicle. Tears are flowing even heavier now. The jeep stops and Mother is nearly to the door. I make my way past Vikter to exit, but I cannot help but feel sad that I am now abandoning him.

"Please don't take my child!" Mother pleads to Vikter over and over again. Tears have flooded her face, too.

His stone face looks really serious now, "You Germans bombed my home in Russia and killed my wife and daughter." There is so much emotion in his voice, and now he is joining in our tears, "Your daughter is my daughter's age before she died, and she looks a lot like her. So I am taking her."

"No! Please I beg you!" Mother's sobbing is too much for me to handle and I know I could never leave her.

"Vikter, I have to stay with my mother. Please!" All I can do is look at him and hope that he sees the fear and sadness in my eyes like I can see in his.

All of a sudden, he reaches out and reluctantly and gives me a salty kiss, tells me he loves me through his shaky voice, and helps me down and into my mother's arms. Just holding each other seems to double our tears, and we both look up to Vikter with thankful eyes. Before we can even press back our cries enough to say anything to him, he is already riding off into the dust and heading for Russia without me.

GRADE SCHOOL
IN TRAMSTOW,
EAST GERMANY

Let the wise listen and add to their learning.

This is a picture of all the students in my school as well as my teacher (left), my principal (right), and me (first row, third child over from the left).

"Sigrid, you had better be leaving for school!"

Here we go again! Jörg is already calling out at me from our room to leave like he does every weekday. But I don't want to go to school. I hate school.

Like every other morning, I head out the door and begin my two kilometer journey to our one-room schoolhouse on the other side of town. Just going to town is a journey in itself from our isolated farmhouse. Normally I walk along this dusty, seldom traveled road and have to squint my eyes tightly even though it isn't a sunny day. Even worse is my circumstance today. It rained last night which means the dusty, seldom traveled road is now a muddy, seldom traveled road spotted with numerous puddles, or as I would like to think of them, landmines. When it is dusty, I just find a tire track and walk in it so my shoes don't fill with dirt. This trick took me a couple of weeks to figure out, but I haven't devised any strategies for avoiding puddles. And this is rather unfortunate considering the cardboard soles of my shoes are beginning to wear out.

Even though the light is starting to break through for the day, I don't think it is going to be very bright, especially with all of this looming haze. All I know is I'm tired and wish that I had somebody to walk with me to school everyday and avoid the landmines with me, but I know that they will come to school later today. Whenever Mother has enough energy to spend time with me at the end of the day, she talks to me and hears my complaints, but most of the time she uses her so-called "tough love" and tells me I need to be strong because we are lucky to be on the farm.

Splash!

Defeated by another puddle. I wish I had magical powers that enabled me to never hit a landmine, but even better I wish my powers would make it so I never had to go to school.

Squish!

With every step, my feet sink into the muddy strand of rolled-out cookie dough and my two cookie cutters push into the dough and leave their mark. Every step is a struggle. It's almost as if the ground doesn't want me to be stepping on it so it is trying to make me trip, but it's the same at school, too. Yes, I am German and so are all of the other students, but me, Jörg, Wolfgang, Harry, and the other kids from the farm are all outsiders at school. We are called "refugees" and not very well accepted.

Stomp!

One landmine avoided! I do have several things I can be thankful for today, despite the soaked earth. At least it is not winter when the snow is up to my knees and the wind blows from every direction, or good thing there are no wild boars or pigs chasing me today . . . karma for pestering the farm pigs perhaps.

Splat!

Finally I can see my quaint schoolhouse. Just a couple more landmines to dodge and I'm there. As I walk past a few boys playing in the saturated yard in front of the school, I can see my teacher through the window preparing our work for the day. How am I to think of doing school work in order to move on and prepare my future when we have all but moved on since the war has been "over"?

Squeak!

Climbing the few wooden, creaky steps that lead to the school and sliding past the door whose hinges are parched for some grease, I can immediately see the clique of girls gathered near the back of the room. One would think that my outfit was inspired by today's weather considering my dull look and the speckles of mud that cover my legs and dress. But these girls . . . wow. Their dresses are as vibrant and fresh as a new spring day.

What's new though? Everyday they have on spotless, beautiful dresses, and everyday I have to wear the evidence of my journey. It doesn't help that I only have two dresses and Mother is allotted to wash them but once a week. From my spot near the front corner, I just watch them talk and laugh as if their main cares in the world are centered on maintaining their dresses and producing a constant smile.

I want to be like that. I trudge through the elements alone daily to sit in a schoolhouse full of people, yet I am so alone. Since we moved from Stettin to Anklam, my family has slidden from well-off and respected because of my father's job in the courts to, well, nobodies. If I am honest with myself I know that it's not so much the journey I take to school that I hate, it's not being accepted.

MY MOST MEMORABLE
CHRISTMAS ON THE FARM

Fröhliche Weihnachten
O Tannenbaum,
O Tannenbaum . . .

Christmas is my favorite time of the year! Being on this farm, Christmas is the one thing that makes me truly happy. I love waiting for the arrival of my Christmas present. I have heard some of the girls at school talk about the multiple gifts that they receive, but I know that Mother has hardly anything now so I am fine with my one present. Charlotte and my cousin, Maria, always send me my present now since we have been relocated, and it's usually a doll of some sort.

Last Christmas Eve, I got to open the gift they sent me, and, to my surprise, it was a real porcelain doll! It was so precious that I couldn't put it down. At night, millions of names would flash across the back of my eyelids as I laid in bed or when I was sleeping. Excitement is an understatement of what I felt when I got my very own porcelain doll. I felt lucky. But eventually, I landed on a name one night as it scrolled over my eyelid. Her name was Heidi.

Heidi was a perfect gift and companion, but this year, something has gotten me more on the edge of my seat than last year. I don't know if this is good and exciting, or if this is really scary. All I know is I'm nervous!

"Better be nice to me because the Weihnachtsmann is coming this Christmas, and if you're bad, he'll spank ya!" Jörg bends over and whispers to me like he's giving me a heads-up and really helping me out.

This has been constant. I feel like I'm on pins and needles. Instead of helping me out, it's almost like he's threatening me. If I ever deny doing Jörg a favor he asks of me, he throws guilt at me. "Well, I hope the Weihnachtsmann doesn't ask you if you've been a good sister this year . . ."

Of course, this leaves me no choice but to comply with his every demand. With Jörg being older and smarter, I learn a lot of important stuff. I do feel like I have a hint about what to do and the Weihnachtsmann that nobody else knows. Maybe I'll get the best present like another Heidi. All I know is I'm going to be as good as I can be and not tell anybody what I am up to . . . . not even Wolfgang.

*　　*　　*

Finally, it's Christmas Eve! I feel like somebody captured a rabbit off the farm and put it in my heart, and now it's hopping around in there like it's never hopped before! Sleep has not been abundant for the last couple of nights, but that doesn't faze me with the nerves I have now.

All day I have been thinking about our impending visitor. I couldn't concentrate on the imaginary game I was playing with Wolfgang earlier, and I was doing such a poor job of cleaning because of my daze that Mother actually excused me from cleaning!

Now we are all gathered here in the family room awaiting the Weihnachtsmann's arrival. This is rare that all families are together and no adults are working, but that's the beauty of Christmas. Most of all though, that tells me that this is a *big* deal if even the adults are here for it.

Creeeeak!

Someone just opened the door, but I feel like everything in me is about to close down. Everything that I've done for the past couple of weeks is flashing through my head.

good . . . good . . . iffy . . .

Nothing too awfully horrible is sticking out at the moment, but I just hope that I don't get a spanking. He's here . . .

"Well, children, who's first?"

The Weihnachtsmann has a deep, somewhat raspy voice, and his crimson outfit is more than I expected. His beard seems to get in the way when he talks, and his eyes are a little shifty.

"I'll go first!"

Not surprisingly, Wolfgang is eager to do it. That's fine with me because I really want to see what happens before I go. So, Wolfgang makes his way over to the holiday visitor and sits on his lap. It seems like the Weihnachtsmann is asking him questions, but I can't hear anything and Wolfgang's answers seem to be brief.

In a snap, Wolfgang is finished and walks away with a small gift and a peculiar grin across his face. Drowning in my nerves, I stand up to catch a gasp of air and paddle over to the Weihnahtsmann's lap. My uneasy feeling is growing and weighs me down; especially with how hard-fixed his eyes are on me. And now, it's time.

"Little girl, I have some questions for you this Christmas Eve." His voice seems louder than it was with Wolfgang.

"Yes, sir," I answer meekly.

"Have you been doing well in school?"

"Yes, sir," my voice is now trembling like there is a wave tossing me in this ocean of nerves, and it's true, I have made good grades and even won some competitions.

"And what about your brother? Have you been good to him?"

Yes, I have! I have been slaving around for him for weeks! But all I can bring myself to say is, "Yes, sir."

"Very well. Merry Christmas!"

He hands me my small gift, and now, with the weight lifted off of me, I freely glide back to my place on the ground. I can't believe that's all there was to it! All of my good behavior paid off and I got away spank-free and with a present to boot!

*　　*　　*

First day back to school since the Christmas break, and it's been quite a smack back into reality. I was happy to see my two new girlfriends who are also refugees, but the monotony of school never ceases to lag on.

To make matters worse, I learned some shocking news today. The Weihnachtsmann, well, he's not real. All of my worrying and nerves were all in vain. I found this out when I got to school and a little later in the day someone from the farm had told about our Christmas experience and visitor. To everyone's amusement, I still believed in the Weihnachtsmann, for I was not aware that he wasn't real!

Who was the visitor at the farm on Christmas Eve? It was Jörg. All dressed up and with a disguised voice I didn't even recognize him. I thought he had just gone to the outhouse for a minute. Nope, it was him, and he had planned it from the beginning. I don't know why I'm shocked though because he usually entertains himself by playing tricks on me, and it makes me sick to think of how much of a kick he must have gotten out of this one. All I know is that when I get back to the farm after school, Jörg better watch out!

SUMMER ON THE FARM

Good news brings health to the bones.

The summer sun could melt you, but the breeze is so soothing. You know, I really don't mind working out in the fields at all. Elfriede says I am old enough to work full-time now that I am on summer break, and at first, to be honest, I was not happy about this.

Yes, I have assisted Mother before, digging potatoes, staking straw, and planting vegetables, but that was when I was younger and thought I was special and privileged to do "adult work". Now, I don't feel the same way about work, but quickly, I whipped myself into shape. Our situation doesn't allow for selfishness; plus, I knew I could make the best of it.

The farmer pays me for my work, and with my newly earned money, I give a little to Mother to help her out and the rest I save. I haven't quite figured out on what to spend my minute sum of money.

Pondering over all of the possibilities of my first financial decision does help to pass the time of my tedious labor.

Today, though, the sun is bright and the breeze that rhythmically sweeps across the farm makes all objects capable of movement sway in harmony. For the first time, our spot of relocation looks beautiful to me.

Like every other day, I string and hang numerous tobacco leaves whose supply seems to be infinite. By the end of the day, my hands will be dry and stiff, but it is all tolerable because I am proud of myself for working for a paying "job".

Maybe I should get a doll . . . no, I still have some from Christmases past. What about a dress . . . what's the point? It will just get dirty. What about . . .

"Hey there, less daydreaming and more work, little girl!"

What do you know? It's Wolfgang gallivanting around the farm, and how kind of him to stop by even though I know he is just going to rub in the fact that I have to work and he doesn't because he's "not old enough".

"Yeah, yeah. What are you up to, Wolfgang?"

"Just got done stealing a sandwich from Elfriede's nephew." As if, despite his young age, he has some greater world knowledge than everyone else, he shakes his head. "So young . . . Anyway, how's work? Seems to me like you're slacking. I wouldn't be surprised if you get fired from this job, too."

He is talking about how Mother seldom lets me get bread from town anymore because by the time I walk all the way back, there are usually just a few crumbs left in my hands. She has never gotten mad at me for it because she knows I am growing and hungry, but it doesn't make me her top choice to employ for the job anymore.

"Actually, Elfriede tells me I'm doing a fine job, thank you. Plus, you're just jealous that you're not earning any money!"

"Jealous? Nope. Not me. But what do you plan on doing with your new riches anyway? I'd sure love a new pocket knife."

As I labor away, Wolfgang is talking so quickly that he's beginning to sound like the chickens.

"I have no clue. I've thought about it, and of course I'm helping my mother out, too, but I don't even know what I want anymore."

"Well, how about something fancy? You're always playing with me and Harry like you're some boy. Get yourself something girly."

He's got a point. I'm a little rough for being a girl even though there are no events on the farm that call for any reason to be fancy, but I still want to have something that sets me apart from the boys . . . . It just came to me!

"What if I get earrings?!"

"What? You mean you want to have some stranger put some holes in your ears?"

"Well, I would have to get my ears pierced to have earrings, Wolfgang."

"You know. That's a pretty good idea. You'll be looking like a fancy girl, but I will agree to your decision on one condition."

Here we go. "What is that?"

"You still have to play with me and Harry and not be afraid of getting dirty or pulling an earring or something when we climb a tree. Deal?"

"Of course it's a deal! There's no way I'm going to just stop having fun."

"Good, Sigrid. I'll go tell Johanna!"

"Not now she's busy! Just . . ."

Too late. He's already off to tell Mother even though her work is probably five times more tasking than my tobacco stringing. I am pretty excited I have to admit though, and I'm glad Wolfgang is excited too. Now I'll probably look more like the girls at school, and, as far as I know, I don't think you can get earrings dirty.

"*Sigrid!!!*"

Already, Wolfgang is sprinting back from his message delivery and pieces of earth and probably some helpless bugs are being kicked back and hurled through the air with his every stride.

"You're going tomorrow!"

"Tomorrow?!" I can't believe it's so soon.

"Yes, the farmhand is going into town tomorrow, so you guys can ride with them."

I'm so excited. Finally, I am considered old enough to work, and, an even better benefit of age, I am going to have earrings. I'm on my way to becoming a real lady.

BACK IN THE HOSPITAL

I was sick and alone and You looked after me.

The pain is almost unbearable today, and I feel like someone is in my throat and slowly sewing it up. The doctors say I have tonsillitis. I have been told to stop complaining because I am next in line for surgery today. I'm scared.

About a week ago, I felt my throat getting extremely sore, so much so that I couldn't even bear to swallow my favorite bread! Soon after, I got a fever and Mother insisted that I go into town to the doctor. A wagon pulled by two horses was brought up to the farmhouse, and I was laid in the back with blankets covering me. There were several of Elfriede's thickest blankets piled over my sick body, but it didn't matter because the chill I felt was incessant. The entire ride Mother comforted me and kept reassuring me, "You'll be okay, Siddi," but I could see the worry mounting deep within her beautiful, bluish-gray eyes because I knew as well as her that there was no way we could afford this.

Once at the hospital, a plump, stern doctor quickly looked into my mouth with a light, took my temperature, and demanded I be transported off to another hospital in a different city that is even farther from the farm to have my tonsils removed. So, with deep concern in her voice (both for me and our financial situation), Mother consented with a brief, "Alright, get my daughter well." We took a rather long train ride and when we arrived at the hospital, she kissed me goodbye, and off they took me. She is not able to visit me; I know she can't afford it. Mother will come and pick me up in two weeks. This fact I know.

And now, here I am. My fever is down, but I would rather have a fever and chills all up and down my body any day than have a throat that feels like it's all scratched-up, swollen, and insufficient because it can't even squeeze down the slickest of foods.

"Sigrid, they are almost ready for you."

Ouch!

The nurse just poked a long needle into my neck, but she quickly explains, "This will make it so you don't feel anything during your tonsillectomy."

So that's what it's called.

"Ma'am, is my neck swollen, too?" I lift my chin into the air so she can really examine it.

She leans down and glances at it and answers, "No, I don't see anything," and she walks away with a chuckle. I don't think it's very funny though.

Well, I have no clue what is going to happen to me, but that shot sure was not a good sign! Most of the other kids on my wing have already had their surgeries, and unfortunately, none of them could eat for a couple of days. What shocked me the most though was their voices disappeared, too. A couple of the boys got theirs back the other night, and now they can play the word games that they used to play at night. I am pretty good at their games, and even though it strains my throat, I often toss out answers. But when these boys' voices were gone, I would see their faces light up during our games, and that told me they knew the answer. Then their mouths would open, and their lips would perform a silent routine. That's when I knew they had lost their voices, and eventually they gave up on the game for awhile.

"Alright, Sigrid Kühl! It's time." The nurse announces that they are ready for my surgery as she approaches me and my gurney with brisk, staccato steps resonating from the cold, hard hospital floor.

Without another word, she is pulling me through the grid of halls, and with every turn, I can feel the soreness of my throat being left behind the corner. Or rather, I can't feel anything. I guess the shot is working.

Finally, we enter the operating room after my gurney is pushed through two swinging doors. I can see the doctor at the end of the narrow room, and he is hovering over a counter and manipulating "doctor stuff" I suppose. Suddenly, not just my throat has lost feeling. My whole body seems out of control, and I am pretty sure my stomach is trying to inch its way up to my throat. No doubt that my face is now as blanch as the walls and my body as cold as this room's personality.

"1 . . . 2 . . . 3 . . . up!"

A couple of nurses lift me into a chair and place a sheet over my body (maybe they noticed how cold I was). The other nurse hands me a white metal bowl, and secures my hands around its base. Now, the doctor who was standing across the room turns to face me, helpless and numb in a chair of seeming doom.

He is suited up in gloves and a coat that brushes his ankles and restricts his every advance. They must have designed this room after him because he looks just as stretched and uninviting as the room. Though he is getting closer, his figure appears smudged, and now I can feel the touch of a sterile hand prodding my mouth open.

In a blur of movements, I can see the doctor is performing some kind of work in my mouth. I wonder what he is doing . . . I look to my left, and there are the two nurses standing with hands clasped behind their backs ready for action. I look to my right, and the contents in the breast pocket of the doctor's coat startle me. I can't look in front of me because the doctor's face is directly before mine, and the concentration in his eyes concerns me. With no other options, I look to the ceiling and pray that everything will be done correctly and quickly!

"Okay," the doctor straightens his long frame and looks at the nurses who seem to know what this means.

With one nurse before me and another to my left, once again my mouth is forced open, but this time my head is pushed down as if I am about to dive into the bowl in my lap.

Plop!

A bloody, round ball rolls out of my mouth and bounces once as it unites with the bottom of the bowl.

Plop!

A second one follows. Keeping my head down but just raising my eyes, I can see the doctor is back at the counter already. It must be over.

Clink, clink, clink . . .

My head still down, a steady flow of blood drips from the corners of my mouth and lands in the bottom of the bowl with a smack to join my two, now homeless, tonsils. The tempo of the blood now seems to me a ticking clock counting down every moment until I can eat, see my mother, and feel normal again.

MY FATHER'S RETURN

(summer 1948)

A house divided against itself will fall.

Lately, the farm has been stirring with anticipation, and I have never seen the women so joyful in their work. It was all sparked by the arrival of the first German soldier back on the farm, Herr Hannemann.

Frau Hannemann, Elfriede, and the rest of his family were not only happy about his return, but they were so thankful because he is an elderly man and not in the best of health before he was drafted. Even though he is higher in age, his family noted that he looked even more rugged and skinny and his old body looked tired all over. The rest of us on the farm didn't know any differently, for we had never seen the farmer before now. His return came as a total shock to everyone, for we have no communication with the soldiers. Now, every wife on the farm is anxious for her husband's return, and they have been working even harder in preparation. I think the real reason they are all working so hard now is because they finally see the light at the end of the tunnel and have gained motivation from that.

His arrival was a couple of weeks ago, and since then, the weather seems to have kicked-up the temperature as we progress further into summer. This heat is making work in the fields more taxing especially since I don't seem to have the energy of the other women. I miss my old job of stringing tobacco on days like this, but it is worth the labor because I get to work alongside my mother now.

Adding to the heat, the gauze wrapped around my head is now soaked with sweat, and it seems to be collecting rays of heat from the sun and trapping them against my head. Just a little over a week ago, I had a major accident. Wolfgang and I were going to get Harry to have some fun, so we made our way up the narrow, wooden stairs that lead to his family's room. That part was fine, but on the way down, my wooden clog shoe didn't quite make a sturdy step on one of the stairs, and down I tumbled. My landing was far from graceful, and I came up with a huge gash that was oozing crimson blood from my left temple. Jörg cried when he saw me, so I am certain it must have been pretty bad. A couple of days later, Mother took me to the doctor, but he said she had waited too long to bring me to the hospital and that I will probably have a scar on my head for the rest of my life. So he simply wrapped me up and sent us home.

The fields' growth has been successful this summer due to favorable weather conditions and our careful tending. This fall's harvest is sure to be bountiful; this impending success serves as my motivation. From the other women, though I still hear hope in every *heave* and love in every *hoe*. Their breathing consists of pleasant releases of air unlike the weighty breaths that are exhaled by bitter laborers, and their weathered faces wear tight expressions of delight, not pain. Often, I look around for encouragement and model myself after these strong women, but currently, their heaving and hoeing has ceased, their breathing paused, and their expressions have gone loose.

"Who do you think it is? Which one?" Harry's mom breaks the silence as she raises her head from her work, but the rest of her body remains frozen in its hunched over work stance.

"Oh, could it be?" another woman interjects, her voice trembling.

All of the women's heads are aimed toward the sandy, dust clouded road that is sandwiched between our two fields, and their eyes are fixed on a distant, slow moving silhouette. Following suit, I also direct my attention to the road's only traveler, and it becomes apparent why so much suspense has fallen upon the group. The traveler is a man clad in the uniform of a German soldier.

I look over at Mother to check her reaction, but her face is just blank as if ready to take on whatever emotion necessary depending on the outcome. It would just thrill her if my father came home, I know that, but I'm not sure if I could share in her joy. How can I let a man who has contributed no positive input in my life step in as my father after so many years of absence?

The soldier has just crossed over from the road and into our field, and though his progress is slow, each step is deliberate. None of the women seem to recognize this man, for he is too old to be any of their husbands. With this realization, the women gradually get back to their work but half-heartedly now.

"Johanna," the soldier stands only a couple meter's distance from Mother, and she suspiciously looks over her shoulder at the bedraggled man.

"May I help you, sir?"

"Johanna, it's me, Erich, your husband."

Mother's hoe thuds to the ground and her body experiences an abrupt jolt at the claim of this man. With a swift turn and a spirited skip, she propels herself at the soldier. Their embrace opens the floodgates, and Mother and this man water the field with their saturated emotions.

Obviously, he must be my father, but I remember a tall, handsome man who exuded his high stature. Haggard, sick, thin, old, and dirty would be how I would describe him now, and I almost cannot come to terms with this new and not improved version of my once revering father. Mother clearly didn't recognize her husband either. It is hard to imagine that I never felt good enough for this man who now looks so lowly.

"Come, let me take you to the house and get you some food." Mother conveys such a nurturing tone toward her returned husband, "Come along, Sigrid."

My father's eyes, once such a piercing, icy blue, now look at me with as much alertness as they can muster in their now dulled version. We have both changed since we last saw each other through the symbolic glass that divided us when I was quarantined. He scans over my new, mature appearance, and by some impulse of nature and emotion, I walk over and hug his frail frame. Hesitantly, he reciprocates and firmly taps his hand between my shoulder blades and somewhat pulls me closer with his other hand. There is comfort in his arms, but something seems to be absent on his part. A certain warmth that I felt from Vikter doesn't radiate from my father.

In a slightly awkward moment, we release from each other's arms. Mother grabs his hand the moment it is freed, and together we make our way to the farmhouse. As my parents walk hand-in-hand, I notice that their interlocked fingers are serving as more than a loving gesture.

My father's strides are choppy and each advance brings a grimace to his gaunt face, so Mother serves as the most loving, supportive crutch any human being could ever want.

As we make our way to the farmhouse, my father's crutch at his left and me strolling along to his right, the dust of the road clouds around us and encompasses our united, almost complete family (Jörg went away to college which will start soon). In spite of the murky air, I can make out a dark spot on his nose, just below the bridge, that noticeably doesn't belong. War has made quite a few physical changes to him. I could have expected the limp, his drained energy is understandable, and I wouldn't have even been surprised if he had shown up with a large scar beveled along his entire forearm. But this post-war addition, a dulled, black object protruding from his nose, I cannot seem to justify or imagine how it could have gotten there.

Curiosity takes over me, "Father," he tilts his head my direction while still leaning his body toward Mother, "what is that dark spot on your nose?" As soon as the words leave my mouth, I wish I was able to swallow them back up, but the air is too dirty so I take my chances.

Straightening his head back to be parallel with the road again, his eyes squint a little harder and his mouth looks like it's preparing to say something uncomfortable, "That's a shrapnel shell, Sigrid."

His voice abruptly cuts-off and his mouth prepares for no more words. For a moment it seems like the air is going to clear and we are going to get a peek into where this man has been and what he has experienced for the past several years (the majority of my life). Instead, it is apparent that he doesn't wish to discuss the matter any further, so I squelch my curiosity and pry for no more details.

Things are going to change. I can just feel it. There is so much that I want to know and learn about my father, and yet another side of me doesn't even care to ever speak to him. For now though, it looks as if the curtain will remain closed on this man's mysteries, and we will just have to discover his experience-altered contents as we all adjust and they naturally unveil themselves.

FAMILY ADJUSTMENTS

But my mouth would encourage you;
comfort from my lips would bring you relief.

One day was all it took for me to realize. I knew that my father's return would drastically change things. It's as if now we are a family that's been placed together, so we need to function like one. We should be living in a house like our old one that is near the city and has flowers draping over the window boxes. My mother and father should be working respectable jobs, and I should be attending a proper school. In the evenings, we should all be gathered around the table with a feast spread out before us, and we ought to be carrying on conversations about our days and laughing and enjoying each other. Instead, we are stuck here on this farm, unable to move on, just trying to adjust.

My father returned alive, but Mother and I are realizing many parts of him died at war. Mother is so happy that she tries to ignore the changes in her husband, but at times her eyes get sort of glassy as she runs by the kitchen to get him some food, and she will just stop for a minute and say, "Things aren't the same, Siddi," and then plaster a smile over her uneasiness as she briskly leaves the room. She has observed all of these alterations that war has performed on him, but I can hardly notice them because I have never held him in as high of a regard.

Despite the current, somewhat pathetic, state of this once highly-respected, distinguished man of the courts, Mother finds my father's recuperation to be progressing smoothly. She takes care of him and waits on him all day, for she just wants him to relax after so many stressful years. Desperately, I think she just wants him to want to be with us and enjoy our new family life.

When Herr Hannemann first arrived and all of the women's excitement began, Mother had begun to set aside a little money every week, but I didn't understand what for. A week after my father's arrival, she pulled out the stash and went to town with the farmer's family. When she returned, she carried in a rich brown violin.

I really didn't understand then. How can we be spending our money on this instrument when we can't even afford a decent amount of food? She could see shock and disapproval all over my confused face, so she hushed me before I nearly woke up my father from his nap and explained, "This will be a good healing source for him. Your father loved music and is very good at the violin."

I know that he is extremely talented (beyond my capabilities), but I still could not justify this indulgence. So when he finally woke up, he spotted the violin leaning against the wall across the room. I watched him straighten up from the bed as a fire sparked in his eyes. He then approached the instrument, picked it up, and then something miraculous happened. Pure, penetrating notes, harmoniously fused to perfection, were conceived as the bow glided across each string and imbued my very being. The room, which was already empty except for me and this musician, somehow became even more still and vacant as a spell took over the room.

It had been so long. I had forgotten this gift he possessed. The music he produced with each flawless stroke of his arm was so beautiful, yet the musician was the opposite. My father's talents mesmerize and disgust me at the same time.

Of the parts of him that died in the war, his artistic ability was not a casualty. He occupies his time painting flowers, playing music, or writing. Just the other day, he presented Mother with a poem about her hair. The entire piece described and raved about my mother's locks, and I could tell she found it romantic.

Whenever he is performing any artistic piece, I just sit on my couch and observe. Watching him reminds me of Jörg which I hadn't even realized how much he was becoming like our father. Before he left for college, he drew a picture of the farmhouse that was so real I felt like I could just step onto the page and head down the path that leads to the front door, dirt and dust rising around me, and walk right in. I really miss Jörg. Since he left, I have been sleeping on the couch in our little room again (because the other beds can only fit one person each). But I am not complaining. The couch is the perfect place for me to nestle, out of the way in the corner, and watch my father and wish I could share in the talent.

Now, as I lay here and ponder the failure of the relationship that was full of potential just a few days ago when my father arrived, I am at peace. From the peak of this haystack, the evening sky, a painting without a frame that is more beautiful than any man could ever create, is all my eyes can fit in. This is where I come when I just want to withdraw and step back from the rapid change within our room. Up here I feel close to God.

I know that He cares for me no matter what and He is the only Father I ever need. Here with Him, I feel comforted, and this is how I know we will not be stuck here in time forever. I talk to my Father, and up on this peak, I know He hears me.

"Father, please take me away from this place. Take me somewhere else, anywhere in the world, if that is what You have planned for me."

A MARRIAGE IN TURMOIL

Although he claimed to be wise,
he became a fool.

We are in the midst of a new war, and it seems worse than the one we experienced. Just a couple of weeks of getting his strength back was all it took for my father to betray the one who has looked after him all along: my mother.

He started seemingly innocent, only walking into town to visit the Gasthaus ever so often. Mother was not bothered by it; in fact, she was glad to see him socializing again. But after a short time, his trips became more frequent, and his frequency eventually stretched to everyday. When he arrives back home, his breathe is always heavy with the stench of alcohol, and he carries himself as the polar opposite of his once high stature. Now he is just a sloppy fool.

Mother tries to reason with him in the most loving way possible (which is her nature), but he just lashes out if she tells him to watch his alcohol intake and denies that he is even drinking much. As my mother tries to talk some sense into this unruly child, I can see the worry on her face drop from concern to helplessness. All of these years of waiting on the farm for her Prince Charming to return from war, and upon his glorious homecoming, he rode a tattered horse. But the prince's title was no longer fitting since Charm was a casualty of war he didn't try to revive.

His advances haven't stopped there though. He started to leave in the morning and wouldn't return until the evening, and eventually he wouldn't be home until the middle of the night. Once he got home, his being completely saturated in alcohol, a full-on battle would begin. Mother would sneak in a slight jab to start things off, but that small advance would detonate a catastrophic explosion from the opposing side. Like a fly on the wall, I would watch it all unfold from my couch, and it seemed like I couldn't stop myself from praying. I had a feeling the warfare would not be brief.

Unfortunately, my premonition was accurate, and the seriousness of this war escalated when Mother discovered that her husband's lengthy, frequent absences are due to an affair. In the midst of his drunken outings, he had developed a relationship with another woman, and he had been spending all of his time that he could have been with Mother and me with this woman and her family.

Hearing this news completely broke Mother's heart. I couldn't help but think how ridiculous it was for her to be heartbroken over a person who didn't even possess a heart. Constantly though, she would say, "He has changed," in a solemn voice or after one of their battles she would whisper, "That's not the person I fell in love with." Still, I wish she would retreat.

Her heartbreak seemed to spark determination, and Mother wasted no time finding out about this woman. She learned from people who have always lived around Tramstow that the adulteress' name is Erika, and she is married with children as well. Erika has a reputation of numerous, strange affairs in town, but why my father would fall into her trap was a puzzle to everyone. Educated and handsome Erich is stooping to uneducated and homely Erika; that is how people are looking at the situation. When he is sober, I think this even puzzles my father, but he seems to be totally under the woman's spell. A few times, he admitted that he was living a destructive life, but for the most part, he just ignores everything Mother says and keeps living with Erika.

Though he is rarely ever home, I despise any minute he spends in our little room. Even when all three of us are in our chamber, I am so alone. There is no one for me to lean on through all of this ugliness. Mother has been drained and has nothing more to give. Jörg has told Mother that she should let our father go even though he still doesn't understand the mess I am in the middle of, and he cannot comfort me from so far away. Adding to my hatred, I feel like a prisoner of war, and nobody knows where I am. When my father is home, he wants me to lie next to him whenever he relaxes in the bed. I never want to, but Mother always insists saying it's good for me to be with my father. Then she goes off and does work around the house while I am left forced to be next to the man I hate. He puts his hands places on me where I know they shouldn't go, and there is nothing I can do or say. He has power over me. I am simply his prisoner. Though Mother is angry with him, she still desperately tries to keep her husband, so I don't know if she is turning a blind eye to what he does to me or if she really does not know. I know one thing though, I could never tell anyone. Regardless of my sufferings, Mother is determined to be a winner because she wants her husband back.

One day I walked into our room and joined Mother sitting on the edge of the bed. Her eyes were fixed on the ground, and I could tell she was biting the inside of her cheek. Even though she wasn't saying anything, I knew that more things were flying around in her head than I could handle. So I broke the silence, "What are you thinking, Mother?"

Her mouth opened with a deep inhale, and her eyes rose to stare across the room through the door. Still, she offered no response. It was apparent that her heart was really hurting, so I just gently stroked her back and leaned my head on her shoulder. A moment later, she spoke, "I have to try everything." I knew she meant it when she said it.

And she did. She seemed to be trying everything, but nothing brought victory. Mother even went and talked to Erika's husband because now my father would stay at their home for days at a time, but, oddly, Erika's husband was not interested in helping or doing anything about his wife's behavior. From there, she began to take matters even further into her own hands. Mother and I started spying on my father. We would even track him down at Erika's house and peek through the windows. We could see her husband sitting alone in the living room, and Erika and my father would be in another room together. It became too much. I know that Mother wanted to know what was going on so that she wouldn't be in the dark anymore, but the reality became grossly unreal.

Today is similar to the day that Mother declared she would try everything to get her husband back. Once again, I am the only one who can attempt to console her. With each stroke on her back, I hope to refill her a little with the love I have for her, but I know that is not enough. Betrayal has left her heart a bottomless pit, so I pray silently as I wait for her to speak. Lately, I have seen her fire slowly dim, so when I asked her what was wrong today, I was not sure what she would say.

Depression has taken her over, for she will not eat and she spends most of her time in bed. Even now, through the mask of worry on her face, she is beautiful. How can this man do this to his strong, lovely wife? And even so, how can my mother want to be with such a selfish, unfaithful man? I must be too young to understand.

Another war started this one, and the battles are too close to home this time. But in both, I am just a powerless victim. The tragic difference that we are facing now is that there is no happy future to reach toward. The war is over, but another has already begun. My father is home, but he doesn't want to be with us.

With these thoughts sinking in, all I can do is hug my mother tightly. Her body limp, she doesn't hug back. She is too devastated to speak, and there is nothing I can say to comfort her. I hate my father right now. Look at what he has done. But I love my mother so much, yet my love is powerless.

TOO MUCH

So the king asked me, "Why does your
face look so sad when you are not ill?
This can be nothing but sadness of heart."

"You should probably get more sleep, Sigrid," Wolfgang says as he swings his leg across his body to kick a dirt clod to the other side of the road.

"Yeah, I should," I respond with a sigh. He's right. I need more sleep, but it has been nearly impossible with all of the fighting and just knowing what my mother is going through. Luckily I have Wolfgang to walk to and from school with me now. It's a nice escape from my family dysfunction every day. He has shown concern like this before, but he has no idea what I am really dealing with.

My grades have been dropping in school and I hardly talk to anyone. Ultimately, I am alone. Mother doesn't care anymore. In school, my eyes are constantly shutting, and I cannot focus. I guess I don't care either. Last night was an especially bad night though. My father came home late, drunk as usual, and he was only there long enough for him and Mother to fight and argue. It was awful. So today at school, my eyes were probably a little heavier than usual.

"*Kühl!!!*" When my eyelids fell again, the principal's shrill voice zoomed to the back of the schoolhouse and blew my eyes open. He then stormed to my desk; his angry face seemed to be blown back from the wind he was creating. I was scared and numb at the same time. Once at my desk, he produced a stick from behind his back and hit me over the head. Every eye in the classroom was wide open and glued in my direction, but as soon as the principal turned around, so did every head.

Wolfgang probably knows I was embarrassed, but my pride has faded and the incident seems so insignificant. I can see the farm now with the sun illuminating the wonderful refuge it has offered me, but all I want to do is be with my mother already. She understands. Even though she has grown quiet and I know she is tired with sorrow and scared from betrayal, deep down she still loves me. After school, the first thing I always do is run to our little room and lay next to Mother and tell her how much I love her.

"I'll see you tomorrow, Sigrid. I better go help my mom get ready for dinner," Wolfgang says before we part ways. He runs toward the farmhouse, his hair flowing in the breeze and his school sack bouncing off of his back with each stride.

I take my time past the fields and Frau Hannemann's flower garden then up the creaky, porch steps, through the door, and into the living room. Harry is playing with one of the younger children, but I don't even say hello. I just head straight to our room.

At last, safe from the world. Anything that can harm me is within my own family, but I know my mother would never do that. I see her resting in bed as usual with her body cocooned in the blankets and her back to the door. Tiptoeing over as not to wake her, I can't wait to join her slumber. One hip sinks into the bed, and I wiggle my body down until I can rest my head on the pillow. Before I lay down, I wrap my right arm around her and nestle my hand within the covers.

Something's not right. The blankets feel wet on my hand.

Cautiously, I stretch my neck to view the other side of her body, and to my surprise, the bed is crimson stained. Mother isn't moving. She doesn't try to hug me back or resist. She is completely still. I am afraid to, but I know what I must do.

I pull back the blankets, and the sight is shocking. Blood is seeping from her wrists and drenching the blankets. How did this happen?

"Mutti! Wake up!"

No response.

"Please!"

Still, nothing.

There are deep nicks on her wrists. Did she do this?

"Mutti, are you okay?!"

Silence.

Dashing out of the room, past Harry and his playmate, and into the kitchen to leave out the back door, I scream frantically, *"Please, help my mother! Anyone, please! She is hurt! Now, please!"*

I don't see anyone's reaction as I rush by. I am on a mission now. I set out back onto the road I just traveled. Running faster than ever, I know just where I am heading. Anger, fear, and sadness are all powering me forward.

We are worse off than during the war. It shouldn't be this way, and there is only one person to blame.

MOTHER'S BREAKDOWN

For they persecute those you wound and
talk about the pain of those you hurt.

Stampeding through town on a mission, people staring at me from every direction and breath now a hard thing to catch, everything around me is an outside blur, totally unaware of my world and what I am going through. Mother is at home unconscious and bleeding in bed without me, and I haven't the slightest clue if she is okay. Nothing is making sense out of the millions of thoughts darting through my mind. Why Mother would do this, I don't know. I always saw her as unbreakable and strong. She still is, but it took an extremely selfish, deceitful person to push her this far.

Sprinting all the way to the unkempt door, my heart is racing even faster than I had to run to get here. This house, its few decorations, the dying flowers hanging from the windows, all of it makes my blood boil. Just being in the presence of such evil, selfish people makes me sick. I never knew I could feel this much hate, but now my mission is almost complete. Here comes the hard part.

Fear, anger, and confusion still urging me onward, my hand, practically involuntarily, raises and raps on the door three solid times.

He had better answer, now . . . .

Again, with more force and double the anger, I pound on the door.

Pause.

I can hear rummaging from within the house and even faint, rising whispers.

I can't take it anymore.

With all of my might, I pound, kick, and scream at the door as if my sheer frustration and hurt will knock it down, dramatically revealing the adulterer and lousy husband, but instead, the door screeches open (not by my forces and shouts). Erika, looking as disheveled as ever, stands in the doorway with a puzzled, empty expression plastered on her face.

"Out of my way!" I shout as I shove her to the side. Past her, then through the living room where her pathetic husband sits alone as his wife proceeds to be unfaithful under the same roof. I storm into the bedroom where my father is sleeping. All of this and he's sleeping?

"Get up! Hurry, get home, now!"

His eyes squint tiredly as he is startled to life as I frantically shake the bed. Though he is obviously shocked, his face still lacks concern, and he remains silently indifferent.

"Mother . . . your wife . . . she's bleeding all over . . ." All of a sudden, my hands, firmly grasping the bed, are hit repeatedly with warm droplets. I'm crying. My cheeks are completely drenched in salty anger, and I continue to plead, "She won't talk . . . something is wrong . . . please!"

In a rare moment, his face displays worry, and I detect a hint of embarrassment. He springs from his shameful bed and looks at me, his blue eyes in total confusion, but I cannot wait on him any longer. I have to get home to Mother.

Again, I storm through the disgraced house and through town. Sprinting down the final stretch of the dirt road, I feel more alone than earlier today. Who am I to lean on, now? Looking over to my left, there is such an ironic sunset about to take place. Amidst all of this hurt and chaos, there is still such beauty around us. The sunset will paint the sky every night no matter how bad life is, and it starts over the next day as soon as it rises.

"Lord, please show me the beauty in this, and help the sun to still rise for us tomorrow."

There is nobody around the farmhouse, but I can hear quite a commotion stirring from inside. Rushing in, I push my way through the crowd of concerned people hovering in my room, and I can see Mother. What a relief! She's okay and her eyes are open, yet drowsy, and her whole body is trembling. The women have surrounded her with an array of towels, ointments, water, gauze, and other things I didn't even know we had. Not even knowing where to start, all I can do is sit next to my mother and comfort her.

The hubbub of the room pauses for a moment as a new person enters-my father. As he enters the room, every eye shoots him a look of disapproval. I can see the disgrace, guilt, shame, and embarrassment in his eyes and worry pursed in his mouth as he beholds his suffering, abandoned wife.

The women return to doctoring Mother back up, and with secret, tear-glazed eyes, my father gently dabs his wife's face with a moist cloth. All I can wonder is if he cries for his hurt wife or, if once again, his tears will prove to be merely welled out of selfish concern.

THE GOVERNMENT COMES KNOCKING

(1949)

Oh my strength comes quickly to help me.

Knock! Knock! Knock!

All of the women look up from their work in the kitchen wondering which lady will drop what she is doing to answer the door. With a sigh, I set down the plate and wipe my hands on a towel and announce, "I'll get it."

Everyone returns to their duties, including Mother. It is good to see her mingling with the other women and working around the farm again. Over the past couple of months, she has recovered nicely from her incident. Her spirits seem to be better, but I think the silent, emotional toll of the whole experience still weighs heavy upon her.

Knock! Knock! Knock!

Impatient, huh?

Scurrying over to the door, my head lags behind a little as I lean back to try and see who our guest is through the window. It's a couple of well-dressed men in suits carrying briefcases big enough to fit practically everything I own.

I swing open the door, only a few centimeters at first, and then all the way. "Hello, may I help you?" My voice squeaks a little, but somehow I am not overly afraid.

"We are looking for Johanna Kühl."

Suddenly, it's as if two bricks are hanging from the corners of my mouth, and my chin is trembling to support them. The load is too heavy to break through to even respond, so I stare blankly at the visitors.

"Is this not the location of Johanna Kühl? Is this not Hannemann's Farm?"

Strength (or maybe fear) empower me to respond, "Yes, it is, and yes, she is here . . . She is my mother."

A moment of silence follows, and then the stouter of the two officers hastily gestures his hands towards the door. They obviously don't care that I am her concerned daughter, so I step out of the way and they enter our farmhouse. The men's presence overpowers the room. Seeing them with their tall, proud statures reeking of arrogance and power granted by the government opens the door to so many thoughts and memories that of which I wish I could throw away the key. For a moment, I stand at the door, frozen, and take in the sight of the two men, side-by-side against the wall, their necks practically sinking into their pompous shoulders, but I quickly thaw to go warn Mother.

"What are the government men doing here, Sigrid?" Harry's mother asks, almost in tears.

Mother turns around from the cupboard with almost no expression on her face. My eyes shift to the different women in the kitchen, searching for an easier way to deliver this news to my currently fragile mother. They stop for a moment on Harry's mother, and then I walk over to the cupboard with Mother still seeming unmoved, almost numb, to the entire episode.

"They are here for you, Mother," still, no response, "They're waiting in the living room."

"Alright."

Harry's mother, displaying signs of relief and also a newly found, compassionate fear for my mother, nearly breaks the saltshaker in her rush to comfort her, but Mother hardly reciprocates. With her brief response, she briskly walks to the other room with a purpose, leaving everyone else speechless with confusion of what's happening and what is to come.

LEFT BEHIND

Do not fear for I am with you.

"Jörg is in jail."

What?

The words ejected from my mother's lips pierce my heart. My brother whom I love so dearly and has been away for such a long time is now suffering thanks again to my father. Our world was shaken (even more than it already was) the day the Secret Service officers interrogated Mother. She was not in any trouble, but that's how we learned that my father had escaped. No longer is he cooped up here in the East. No, he is free in the West, and we are stuck here.

The officers had come to find out what route he took to get to West Germany, demanding every detail be handed over, but she didn't even know that he had planned to leave. He never came home the night he supposedly escaped, but that was not an unusual thing. Mother was interrogated for a long time, and all of the women in the kitchen tried their hardest to stretch their ears to catch every detail. Still, we couldn't hear much, but later she told me everything.

My father escaped to freedom, and he took Erika and her family with him. Not us.

We are still in shock and hurt. He had not been acting differently, there were no signs that he was devising plans, he never packed anything, and he never even said goodbye. His whole intricate plan (which had to have taken months to work out the details) had been done completely behind his wife's and daughter's backs, and in the end, he did not even consider his real family.

"Is he okay?" I reply expecting Mother to offer reassurance. After the Secret Service was convinced that Mother had no knowledge of my father's escape, they started to dig into Jörg, and it turned out that he had been informed of the whole plan in detail (another piece of evidence of my father's lasting favoritism towards my brother).

"I think he will be, Siddi."

Relief.

"Your brother is smart though. Very smart . . ."

"How so? He is in jail."

"Well, he did not lie. He told them that he knew the path your father and Erika's family took to cross over, but he would not reveal specific details immediately. That's why he is in jail, and he will be out by tomorrow. Thank the Lord," she looks up and blows a kiss to the sky.

Apparently I am not as smart as Jörg because I still don't get it. "So, why is that good?"

"Because he is not cooperating fully with the authorities, he is in jail, but Jörg only has to stay one night because he just told them the rest of the plan," Mother has an almost crazy grin on her face as she shares these details with me, "Jörg purposely withheld the certain day and times of each move they took because he wanted to wait until they would be safe in the West. By now, he knows that they have had enough time to make it, and there is nothing they can do to get your father."

My brother always was sharp. "Wow," I say halfheartedly. While I am amazed at my father's escape, Jörg's smarts, and their overall collaboration, I mainly feel overwhelmingly hurt. My poor mother and I were in the dark once again, and ever since we came to this farm, we have been alone. Even after the war and once my father returned, we were still alone, neglected. We were more alone when he was here than when he was at war. When he was gone, Mother held on to the hope of being reunited with her providing husband, but that ended up to be nothing but a teasing fantasy leaving her spirits totally empty. This time, he chose to leave us, and it's for good. With all of this talk of escaping to freedom, I can't help but feel left behind.

HOPE INTO ACTION

Do nothing out of selfish ambition or vain conceit,
But consider others better than yourselves.

For two years, life has been carrying on for Mother and me. There is still work to be done on the farm and school to be attended. Not much has changed here. Ever since we were relocated and our freedom was taken, it's hard for the families to move out of the farmhouse and regain their independence. We have been left with no choice but to exist together, and thankfully we have surpassed that and almost become family by looking out for each other. Even with our new family, Mother and I remain incomplete. We are stuck here with no options while my father and Erika's family are free in the West. Not a day goes by that we don't feel abandoned, but I think it only feeds Mother's flame.

For two years, my father has not sent us any money to help support his wife and children. We seldom hear from him, but we get most of our information from Jörg. My brother enlightened us that my father, Erika, and her family were all living together in Neustadt, and he had his job all lined up before he even left East Germany. Back he was on his pedestal, where he was before the war began, working in the jurisdictional system. Once again, he has two secretaries running around for him and people showering him with respect everywhere he goes. I can just imagine this prestigious wolf parading around in sheep's clothing, fooling everyone into thinking he is an honorable man. In reality, he left his family and has done nothing to help us since running away in the middle of the night two years ago.

Though the cloud of my father looms over me, I will not let it rain on my success. Academically, I have excelled. Socially, I have better relationships. Overall, I am happier knowing that he is far away, yet I know that something is missing. I continue to pray to God about the circumstances in my life, and I trust where He will lead me.

Mother, however, has an even darker cloud constantly hanging over her, and it tends to frequently rain guilt, fear, sadness, and anger on her life. She feels guilt for, well, me I guess. For having me witness what I've witnessed and endure the things I've endured. I know she's scared that we will never get off of this farm or out of East Germany, and we will never be free. Often times I see her tearing up, for it is almost as if she is grieving over the loss of her husband. He was a belated war casualty. Most of all though, we share in our anger. She channels hers more discreetly than I do mine. While others may lash out when they are filled with animosity, she tucks away her feelings and works feverishly to achieve whatever it takes to mend the issue.

For the past two years, ever since we discovered my father's whereabouts and financial situation, Mother has been sending him letter after letter pleading for help. She has tried everything to get him to support his wife, daughter, and son, but he rarely responds and never follows through with Mother's wishes. I'm not sure if it's merely the financial strain that makes her so desperate (though I know we are struggling), but knowing her, she just wants to remind him who his real family is.

So for two years, she has sent numerous letters, and for two years has been ignored. Finally, a few weeks ago, I saw Mother tearing up a piece of parchment with each harsh stroke of the pen, and noticing my curiosity, she informed me that she was notifying my father's work place that he is making no attempt to send for us and has not provided anything for us financially. She introduced herself as Erich Kühl's wife and mentioned his two children. Only a week later, the higher officials wrote her back saying they had no idea that we are still in East Germany or that any of this is going on, for he had led them to believe that we were living with him.

When I read that, my blood boiled.

The officials said that, in order to maintain the clean image of the higher courts, they do not allow such behavior from their employees, so they have given him an ultimatum: send for your family or lose your job.

Unfortunately, I know what he will choose. He will send for us, but it is only out of the love he has for his job, not for us. That encouraging letter came a week ago, and we should be hearing from my father any day now. Mother and I have not heard anything yet, but I can feel that change is on its way and the wheels in Mother's head are spinning faster than ever now.

OUR DANGEROUS ESCAPE
TO WEST GERMANY
(1951)

I will instruct you and tell you
the way you should go.
I will watch over you.

"Did you check the bottom drawer, Siddi?" Mother calls from the living room.

"Yes, Mother. You had already gone through it."

It's here. Our final day on the farm has passed, and it's chaos. I don't even know what to feel. I'm sad to leave yet happy to move forward, but right now, I am trying to fathom what lies ahead.

Much planning and preparation have gone into today. Elfriede and Mother have been working out the details for weeks, and I still do not quite understand everything that will happen. The one thing that I know and have known that I must do is to, under no circumstance, talk about this to anyone. Since my father escaped and was found out, we know that neighbors, best friends, or anyone could be watching and turn us in and even the Hannemans for assisting us. The Eastern European soldiers have had special training to have a sensitive eye for any travelers who act or look a little suspicious.

Imagining the consequences of our journey is terrifying. Stories of people put in prison, sent away to labor camps, or even killed have been flooding the news and trying to drown us in fear. Despite the danger, one thing is for sure. We will begin our journey tonight, and we will escape.

I walk into the living room with a few articles of clothing draped over my arms. "I found these in the back of the wardrobe. Where should I put them?"

"Just leave them! We have way too much as it is. We don't need it. We simply don't need it," her voice drifts off as she shakes her head and looks at the floor.

The whole day she has done nothing but prepare for tonight. She weeded through our belongings choosing minimal items, stuffing them into our suitcases and throwing the rest behind like unwanted baggage. We can only take very few belongings so we are not suspicious on the train. Over the past seven years, we did not accumulate many items, so to her, this is easy compared to when she had to choose what to take when we were forced to leave our house. Arrangements were double checked, and particulars were smoothed out.

"Anytime now, Sigrid! Hurry!" Mother is beginning to get nervous since our ride will be here any minute.

One final scan of the room. So many memories . . . not all pleasant but close to my heart. This is where I grew up, and now our dreams are allowing us to grow out. Turning around and walking out of the room for the last time, I join Mother and the Hannemann family in the living room. They are all holding hands with their heads bowed, and Mother glances up and motions her head in a circle to cue me in. The Hannemann family and Mother believe in prayer, and so do I. This is all we really need for this journey.

Frau Hannemann leads, "Lord, thank you for giving us the time we had with Johanna and her family. Make them strong for what lies ahead. Bless their journey, and cover them with your safety, Father, as well as our family. Thank you, Lord."

In unison we pray, "Amen."

Heads around the circle all raise, and I can see a wet glisten in every eye. We will be missed, and we will miss them. It is hard, but Mother is determined to give herself and her daughter a better life. None of what's about to happen would be possible if it wasn't for this family.

As hugs continue to circulate the room, the sounds of rickety wheels, horse hooves, and churned earth penetrate the walls and alert everyone. No one need say a word, for the time has come. Quietly, Mother and I grab our belongings and step outside to the wagon waiting for us that Elfriede arranged. Before we walk through the door though, Mother pulls out our two plane tickets from West Berlin to Frankfurt Main Airport that my father sent just to double check, and then she slides them back into her pocket.

Everyone files out as well to see us off being carefully quiet so no one else on the farm is awakened to our getaway. Mother loads our suitcases into the wagon and covers them with our down comforter (the one thing Mother irrationally could not part with). A few silent waves but mainly sad faces entertain the night scene, and like that, we're off.

The wagon jolts forward, and we are on our way. First stop on our escape to freedom: the train station. From there we will go to East Berlin to stay with Tante Lieschen. If and when we are asked why we are traveling there, Mother can honestly say that we are going to visit her sister. I'm not sure how much she and Mother have communicated and planned out our next move from there. It would be risky to write too much about it, but I know Mother has something in mind and Tante Lieschen is a smart woman.

Just as we entered this place by wagon, so we leave it. Part of me sees myself walking to and from school as we travel the road under the night sky, and I also see me frantically sprinting down the dirt path to get my father once again from Erika's house. That alone makes me want to kick the horses into a gallop and get us out of here to a fresh start. I keep turning to see familiar sights fade into the distance as we move forward, but Mother's eyes are fixed tightly on the road before us.

Finally I see the lit train station, and we pull up. Mother thanks our driver more than five times as we unload and leave the wagon. Onward we go, Mother with our train tickets in hand. Weaving through the station, I follow her like a lost puppy, but I know that she is the mastermind and I just have to follow her lead. We board the train, and we're off again.

Another step forward.

Everything feels surreal encompassing the mystery of this truly fateful night. There is buzzing about the train cabin, but the bubble surrounding Mother and me seems to be filled with stark silence. German, Russian, and Polish soldiers are scattered throughout the train and continue to check identification cards and ask various questions about passengers' reasons for traveling and their destinations. I cannot help but be afraid because I overheard Elfriede telling Mother about the power these soldiers possess while on the train. They can do whatever they desire with us. Privacy is a thing of the past in East Germany, and it continues to get worse.

Screech!

Every back peels off its chair with a sudden whip forward and, with a force from the opposing direction, is thrown against it again. The train is silent except for the thudding of passing soldiers' boots, but the fear and confusion on every passenger's face speaks volumes. Looking out the windows, there is no station in sight, and we certainly have not reached our destination yet.

"Everyone," a soldier with bold, dark features and broad shoulders barks from the front of the train, "evacuate the train orderly. Row by row. Now!"

UNEXPECTED DETOUR

We are hard pressed on every side,
but not crushed.

Herding out of the train one-by-one following the head soldier, I find myself sandwiched front and back by frightened passengers. The night sky is black velvet studded with diamonds, and the moon is even brighter here than it shown on the farm. A quick chill surges through my body, a product of the fusion of the nighttime breeze and the distress building inside of me. I survey our unofficial destination, but I am left only more clueless. Desolate fields and shaggy grass surround us on all sides. There is not a building in sight, but the soldiers seem to know exactly where we are.

A low murmur blankets our huddle and frightened eyes are now looking towards God. Nervously, I rub my hands against my thighs, partly for warmth and partly to calm my nerves. From behind, I feel someone attempt to grab my hand, but I do not turn around to see because there are so many people accidentally bumping into each other in this chaos. Again, I feel another attempt, but this time it is successful.

"Excuse me. Sorry, sir, I need to get through."

I peer over my right shoulder, too afraid to completely turn around, and I am relieved to see it is Mother fighting her way through the packed bunch to be next to me. Somehow we got separated in the evacuation.

"Mutti! What is going on?"

"Are you okay? Don't worry, dear, we will be fine. Just do as we are instructed."

I just nod and squeeze her hand a little tighter. Within our clasp, I can feel her trembling. Despite her brave speech, I know she is scared, too.

"This way!" The head soldier commands as he points to the opposite direction of the train. "Stay together, and stay quiet!"

So we begin to walk away from the train and further into the unknown. Soldiers are stationed at various points on the perimeter of our cluster to prevent runaways, but I don't know where I would run to even if I could break free. Because of the tall grass, we literally have to march along with the soldiers, lifting our legs high and pressing onward in order to keep up with the pace. It may be the dead of the night, but my senses are as awake as ever. I am prepared to do whatever I am told or react however I must to survive and protect my mother.

Approaching an area loosely populated with trees just bordering the field, I begin to see lights.

There must be something back here.

Sensing a possible end to our march, I tug Mother's arm gently, being careful not to make any noise. I don't know why I did because I'm sure she can see the lights and has the same hunch, but then again, I am not sure of much anymore. She squeezes my hand and glances at me out of the corner of her eye for a second, but she quickly returns her focus to the path ahead.

Twigs snapping beneath our marching feet create the only noise to break the eerie, forced silence until suppressed gasps barely seep out of every traveler's mouth upon the newly beheld sight. A large brick building emerged through a group of trees and proves to be the source of the lights. Obviously abandoned, weeds and vines climb the outer walls, and bits of crumbled bricks are scattered around its base. Now standing only a couple of meters from the building, its scale is more evident. We are ants next to a haystack.

A couple of soldiers lunge their bodies against wide, rusty steel doors so that we can all enter. Without any instruction, we follow the soldiers into the dimly lit building. One soldier returns from around the corner and gestures some intricate signal to the head soldier.

"Alright, everyone find a place to settle, and cooperate."

This doesn't make sense.

Totally confused, we all shuffle around the corner where the soldier had come from, and we enter an enormous room filled with nothing but people. Here I thought we were the only ones out here in the middle of nowhere, but this room is already brimming with hundreds of Germans. Mother and I stand in shock for a moment and survey the scene. Then we proceed to find a spot in the crowded mess.

Stepping over sleeping people, scooting past restless toddlers, and walking around huddled families, we make our way through the room until we find a space on the floor big enough for the two of us. Like everyone, we sit down on the cold, dirty floor and kind of look at each other as if to say, "Now what? Why are we even here?"

"It's been five days," an elderly woman close to Mother lifts her head from rest to say.

"Pardon me?" Mother and I are not sure what the woman means. Five of what or since what?

She juts her head out and closer, "It's been five days since I left our train, and all I have done is lay here."

"What have they been doing? Do you know?"

"Well they come around and pull people out," she pauses to yawn, but I'm not so sure that she isn't trying to hide tears, "Then they interrogate them, search them, and decide their fate."

I can almost see Mother's heart beating out of her chest.

"So what do they do . . . umm . . . what do you mean 'decide their fate'?"

"I'm not sure entirely. If you pass, no worries, you will get to board your train when your group is done, but those who don't pass don't leave. Who knows what is done with them," the woman's eyes look tired, but she stretches them to look at Mother. She must see the sheer terror welling up in my mother's bluish-gray eyes because she quickly switches the mood, "But I'm just waiting my turn. They should bring some bread out soon though . . ."

The woman rolls over and returns to her slumber, but it is evident that Mother will not do much sleeping tonight. I scoot a little closer (if that is even possible), and rest my head on her shoulder. She is not always the most affectionate person, but I know deep down she needs comforted.

"We have too much to lose," Mother says in a surprisingly steady voice, "Once we get past this, and we will, we will be one step closer. All of the plans are in line, and God will provide. Siddi," she shifts away to look at me straight on, "we will be free."

OUR PLAN

I know the plans I have for you.
Plans to prosper you and not to harm you,
plans to give you hope and a future.

Tante Lieschen, and her granddaughter, Karin.

"Welcome! Oh my! I'm just . . ." Tante Lieschen, who was waiting for our arrival at the station, greets us with hugs and kisses. Seeing their faces next to each other, even a stranger would know that they are sisters.

The sight of a loving family member is refreshing after a week in limbo. Mother was interrogated and, thank the Lord, we were released and sent on our way to East Berlin. Unfortunately, the kind elderly woman next to us was taken for interrogation on our second day there, and we never saw her come back to gather her things.

"It is so good to see you!" Mother says with a widely-spread smile, but it quickly shrinks and I can see she is ready for business.

Tante Lieschen slightly shakes her head and her gray hair barely moves underneath her hat. She understands my mother's signal. "Alright, ladies, this way."

We pick up our things, follow her lead, and board the U-Bahn. After a fairly silent ride, we exit the U-Bahn and find ourselves in the hub of East Berlin. Tall buildings, nothing like the ones of Anklam, swallow us up, and the rushing flow of people forces us to keep moving. Still following Tante Lieschen, we turn corner after corner and cross street after street. I don't know how she can navigate through the busy streets and remember so many twists and turns, but something is strange about these city streets and sidewalks. Even though I have never been in a city this grand, I know that the mood should be different. Many people are all around traveling by foot to shops and businesses, but it is almost silent except for some stale street noise and jingling bells as customers enter shops.

Smack in the middle of East Berlin (or so Tante Lieschen tells us) we arrive at her apartment complex. This is the largest apartment complex I have ever seen. I didn't even know so many people could live this closely together! Thankfully, her apartment is not very high up.

Tante Lieschen wraps on her door, and we wait anxiously to get inside the concealed safety. A girl only a couple of years older than me answers the door with a forced smile on her face. She steps to the side to let us all in, and after setting her things down, Mother embraces the girl.

"Sigrid," Tante Lieschen holds out her hands about to present this stranger to me, "this is my granddaughter, Karin." We smile at each other from a distance, and then she struts over and gives me a hug. "She lives here with me," Tante Lieschen says grinning at Karin, "Please, have a seat."

Mother, Tante Lieschen, and I take a seat at their round dining table in the middle of the room with a petite chandelier hanging over it dimly lighting the tiny apartment. Karin leaves to another room and takes our suitcases with her.

"I know we briefly talked about it in our letters," Tante Lieschen says, her voice an octave lower and very business-like, "but I have an escape plan for you. It may not be a quick getaway, for it will take weeks, but I think it will work."

She pulls a map out of a drawer and spreads it out on the table. Obviously she has really thought about this because the map is covered with markings. Mother had told me that her sister knew Berlin well. As she walks Mother through the map, I can see that she knows every route of the street cars, buses, and U-Bahn. Her detailed descriptions of the routes we must take surpass simple street names and cardinal directions. She knows every shop, street beggar, and soldier we will pass. Tante Lieschen even informs Mother of a few people she knows are "safe" and have helped others escape to West Berlin.

"Where exactly are we headed?" I ask, for Mother has never fully versed me on the key points of our plan for my own safety.

"We have relatives in West Berlin," she concisely answers.

I had known that we were going to sneak to West Berlin, but I never knew we had family over there. "What relatives? Have I met them before?"

Mother seems slightly irritated with my questioning and simply responds, "No, you have not. They are distant relatives, but nevertheless, they have agreed to be our checkpoint there."

Fair enough. I don't need to know everything as long as we will be free.

"Every day, you must follow this route and know it like the back of your hand so you do not have to ask anyone on the street. You have to look like you belong and know what you are doing. Do not draw any attention to yourselves," she says with a grave expression, "Go straight to the train station. Taking bags of clothing across the border is a sure way to land in prison or a labor camp, so you will dress in layers but not too many in case you are searched."

I can see Mother taking mental notes, and I am getting more nervous and excited with each precise instruction.

"When asked why you are going to West Berlin, say you are buying clothing or a special food item. Any other reason will not be worthy, and they will send you home, or worse. Once in West Berlin, do not make your visit lengthy, but don't make it suspiciously short either. First go to your relatives' house, and leave your extra layers of clothes. Then, it may be wise to buy something small to avoid contradiction," her eyes are still staring at the map and following the outlined routes as she speaks as if they will come to life at any moment, "You must always come back to the East no matter what. They keep track of everyone who passes through the station, and some days the different soldiers at the train station may be more hesitant in letting you go over. Don't push them. Just come home, and we will try again the next day."

Mother is shaking her head and also staring intensely at the map like she can literally soak it all in through her eyes. "Wonderful. I will always come back because I am not losing everything we have again," is all she can say about it until she feels the need to address further concern, "What about the neighbors? We are surrounded."

I do not understand. Yes, there are people living practically on all sides of us as well as many other tenants we will pass daily, but what does that have to do with our plan?

"I am not sure about the neighbors," Tante Lieschen sighs, "We cannot be too cautious-"

"Why? What's wrong?" I interrupt out of curiosity and paranoia. Here I thought we were safe in this apartment, and now I am not so sure.

"They could be spies, Sigrid," she continues, "The government pays people, not to mention scares people into turning in anyone they think is acting suspiciously or does not agree with the government. These spies live everywhere, and they are normal people. I say I am not sure because I don't want to judge anybody, but I know that some of them do work for the regime and cannot be trusted." Anticipating my next question, she answers, "To avoid suspicion, play the role of visiting family, and act confidently. You should be fine because no one here knows about Erich."

Just hearing his name in the context of having already escaped (without us) visibly irritates Mother. But I find comfort, and almost a feeling of revenge, in knowing that now we have a plan and we are also going to be free . . . even if he didn't want us to be.

FIRST SIGHT OF FREEDOM

How awesome is the Lord Most High.

"Are you sure there is nothing suspicious in your bag?"

"Yes, Mother."

"And you remembered your-"

"Yes, of course."

"And how many-"

"Only three layers Mother. I think we are set," I say trying to calm her jitters before we embark on our first trip to West Berlin, "If we just follow Tante Lieschen's plan, everything should go smoothly."

Biting her bottom lip in concentration, she walks through the apartment door, and I follow her out of our safe house and into the unsheltered world. Though Mother is teeming with nerves, I notice a carefree smile from time to time accompanied with a lilt in her step as we make our way through the streets of East Berlin. She grabs my hand as if we are strolling leisurely through town, but then she quickly squeezes my hand and shoots me a glance.

I get it.

She is really getting into our role. We have to be the visiting relatives, and like Tante Lieschen said, we have to look confident. I must say, Mother is doing a fine job at this considering how profusely her palm is sweating. Nevertheless, she is navigating these streets like she has walked them for years. Tante Lieschen drilled her well.

"This way, Sigrid," she says calmly as we turn our final corner to get to the train station, not walking too quickly or slowly.

I try to relax my face and play along. This trip is only our first of many to come, and I need to get this role mastered. For some reason, I just feel dazed. We are starting our journey to a free life, and I don't know what to expect. Our journey entails traveling forward every day and then digressing back, yet coming back is actually moving us forward. I don't know what to think of it yet. Once I see freedom, will I be able to make myself come back?

"And . . . that's our train," Mother says pointing ahead and walking on.

Onward we go, making our way through the station and the masses of people filling it. Looking around, there are a variety of people. I can't help but wonder if the people with big smiles are trying to cover something as well or if the ones with worried eyes are up to the same plot but are too fearful to bother.

Before we can approach our train, one of the many soldiers patrolling the station approaches us. "Where are you traveling to today?"

For a split second, my mother is startled out of character but quickly recovers, "We are going to West Berlin for the day," she says quite smoothly, but seeing that this is not enough for the soldier (as evidenced by his raised eyebrow), she quickly inserts, "Umm, we are just wanting to purchase some special food."

Anxiously awaiting his reply, we don't have to squirm too long, "The train is that way," he directs us to his left, "You may go board now."

"Thank you, sir," she tries to say in a controlled but extremely relieved voice.

Boarding the train, I cannot help but get flashbacks from our last train ride. Being searched is scary and a bit humiliating, but I am getting more used to it and am able to put it out of my mind for the reward is worth more than the worrying. Without too much delay, we are off, and I only hope that we won't stop again until we pull up to the border and walk into West Berlin. This time, I grab Mother's hand first. Her sweating has relented, but I can still sense the tenseness in her grip. I want to tell her how well she is doing and explain my worries about seeing West Berlin, but I remember what Tante Lieschen said. Anybody around us could be a spy, and I don't want to ruin all of Mother's hard work because of my petty issues.

One soldier in particular has been pacing the train, up and down the aisle, the entire ride. His uniform is crisp, his boots polished, but his face seems to be disconnected from his dressed up persona. He needs to shave some patches on his cheeks, his eyes are like that of a droopy puppy dog, and his bottom lip seems tormented from nervous biting. Like my father, he could be a pathetic man granted authority by the uniform, yet this naturally weak being has been transformed by government intervention and is now powerful enough to instill fear in every passenger. Or perhaps his eyes appear sad and his lip tormented because he has no say in the matter, and he is forced to carry on with his duty. I guess my father has actually taught me something. Soldiers, though seemingly daunting, are only human. It is the government that I should really fear when the day is done.

Screech.

The pacing soldier clutches the back of a seat as the train comes to a halt. He steps out of the train and mans the door as passengers begin to file out. I can't believe we crossed the border that quickly. All along, I have been fairly close to freedom yet so far away. We did it. We are in West Berlin.

Immediately I notice the difference. The people seem cheerful, and the overall mood is brighter. Directly upon leaving the station, I am pretty sure I can see heaven. Little stands and shops line the streets, each offering delicious sweets and foods (even ones I have never seen before). I think my eyes just grew bigger than my stomach.

Seeing my large eyes (and probably hearing my rumbling stomach) Mother offers, "Sigrid, I know that Tante Lieschen said to stop here second, but just this once—and don't get used to it—but just this once, you can pick something out now."

I do not even know where to begin! I scour every shop and stand, feasting my eyes upon chocolates, candies, and fruits of the most vibrant hues. None of these treats were ever available on the farm. The floating smells of pastries and sweets in the air is almost too much for me to handle, not to mention the aroma of freshly baked bread wafting from the corner bakery. So much to choose from and so much to learn, but I have decided what I want. I have never had one, and it is in Mother's price range.

"Mother, I'll try the banana," I decide, devouring the entire fruit stand with my eyes.

"Alright, Siddi. Anything you'd like."

She pays the vendor as I select the largest, brightest yellow banana I can find. The only problem is, I am not sure how to eat it. Seeing my confusion, Mother snatches the mysterious fruit out of my hands and peels back the hard, outer layer.

"There you go," she says handing it back with a *real* smile on her face this time.

"Thank you, Mother," I smile back and take a small bite at first just to make sure.

Wow!

What a wonderfully delicious piece of food. This only makes me wonder what else I have been missing out on for all of these years, but for right now, I will just savor this banana. I did not expect freedom to taste this good.

DANGER

You are my Hiding Place.

"It isn't safe anymore," Tante Lieschen says at yet another serious, night meeting. Her dark-rimmed eyes and sullen expression give away the toll our escape has had on her, but she loves us too much to ever complain.

"So what do we do?" I ask before Mother can get it off her lips.

"Change it up. The new laws they've established make crossing the same checkpoint everyday dangerous, but there are several checkpoints we have to choose from," she answers matter-of-factly with her hands clasped before her on the table.

"Now we will just take different routes," Mother practically repeats, her voice faintly drifting off.

We have made several trips back and forth to West Berlin, and though we have gotten better at "playing the part", it is always scary. Typically, we wear a few layers, I may have another purse stuffed inside of the purse I carry, and it is not uncommon for me to wear a scarf around my neck as well as one around my head. We are like ants carrying food away on their backs from a picnic and taking it to their home, but we always come back to get more. Anything it takes to get the job done, but there are days when we are denied entry. On those days, we simply retreat back to the apartment and wait for tomorrow.

Now, it is getting even more complicated. New laws have thrown a kink in our plan, so no longer will we be able to take our route with little to no thought and just worry about being searched, denied entry, or worse. Now we will have to take a different route every day, maneuvering our way through this foreign city with peril lying in wait around every corner. Luckily, my loving aunt is already systematically thinking ahead of the system so that we can override it and succeed.

"Yes," Tante Lieschen shakes her heavy head is dismay, "you'll have to."

It takes only a moment, a good look at the map (a new staple of the dining table), and she is suddenly rejuvenated.

"There are several options we have to avoid suspicion," she reassures as her scrawny finger traces in every direction over the map, "Johanna, it will be imperative that every night you and I sit here, and I will help you study your path for the next day."

Mother is now leaning so far over the table that I think she is trying to dive into the map.

"This city is big, but suspicion is on the rise. The number of spies is increasing by the hour because the government has upped the incentives for turning in people like us."

She rubs the back of her neck, releasing the tension at the peak of her spine and transferring it to that already filling the room.

"We cannot be too careful. I will have to drill you until you know every street name and corner. And Sigrid," I perk up surprised that part of the conversation is actually directed toward me for the first time.

"Yes, Tante Lieschen," I respond showing my attentiveness and readiness for responsibility.

I want to help in our great escape.

"You should at least sit with us as we go over them. It wouldn't hurt for you to have an idea of where you are headed in case something would happen."

"Yes, ma'am."

I feel honored.

My self-glory is short-lived, and the conversation shifts away.

"These new routes will require different methods of transportation. The U-Bahn, street cars, buses . . ."

"How will I afford all of this?" Mother sighs, making her lungs as empty of air as her purse of money.

"Some of it can be avoided, but I must warn you that it will require a lot more walking."

"Well then walk, we will!"

I am already dreading it.

"Very well," my aunt diverges the conversation to evade my mother's financial concerns, "None of it is looking good. The government is tightening its grasp more than ever, but the stakes are too high at this point. You have made it this far, we cannot let them scare us into defeat."

"No, we cannot," Mother chimes in practically foaming at the mouth with determination; "We just have to stick to the plan and pray. There are scary things happening that we could never be prepared for, so we just have to keep faith and let Him lead us to freedom."

Sitting in such a dark room only lit by a chandelier whose bulbs need replaced and flickering candles dilating sporadically on the walls, I never thought my outlook could be so bright.

ALONE IN A STRANGE WORLD

I will never leave you nor forsake you.

"Thank you so much," Mother thanks her sister as they have a teary embrace, "You risked your lives for us, and we never could have done this without you."

Karin and I release from our hold, and now it's my turn to hug Tante Lieschen as she replies with a quivering voice, "I love you both, and I want you to be free," she seems to regain composure and finishes with a smile, "I had to do it."

Mother lovingly strokes her sister's shoulder as she tries to convey the utmost gratitude, but we both seem parched for words.

After nearly a month, we must leave, this time it's a one-way trip taking our last possession, our down comforter. Hesitantly, we walk through the apartment door for the last time. Too afraid to look at them for a final time because of any neighbors who may be watching, our heads stay stiffly bolted straight on our bodies, and we hear the door shut behind us.

I really wanted to look back.

Sadness overwhelms me for a brief moment as I reflect on the last month we spent with my aunt and how grateful I am to her. She was truly the mastermind of our plan, all the way down to the last detail that we must complete today.

Making our way through these streets on our final journey, I cannot help but feel a little afraid. The town has chilled over even more since our arrival. At first, it was slowly being drained of life, but now someone has pulled the largest plug, freedom, and all vitality is gone leaving the city and its people vacuous. These streets may have grown to be familiar but they never grew to be friendly, and I no longer feel welcome here anymore.

We arrive at the station and board the train with little difficulty during the routine search by the guards, but things are a little different. This train will only lead us to another train. Our strategy has changed because it is now forbidden to crossover to West Berlin. Every crossing point has been closed off, and they have even started building a wall that will divide East and West Berlin. Before, I had seen East Germans who had gotten so desperate that they would swim across the Spree River between East and West Berlin, and right there in the water, I saw them get shot. Now, I have seen people, even more desperate than before, try to climb over the barbed wire fence barrier only to be captured by watchful soldiers who guard the border day and night. I even know people who are trying to dig near the fence to create an underground passage to come out on the other side. None of these escapes are very successful. The few who have made it have been captured and suffered brutal consequences.

The Spree River.

This is the main reason Tante Lieschen had devised a more discrete plan for us that required day-by-day planning and the aid of the underground radio. This secretive station, dedicated to helping people like us, has helped us stay informed of new laws, the best routes to take, and even a special underground U-Bahn. Conductors of this underground operation are literally giving train rides to freedom. East

German passengers, like us, board the train, and then the ride goes a little further than it's supposed to—all the way into West Berlin. Once there, the conductor will stop the train, let everyone unload, and head back to East Berlin. The operators of this secret railway are trying to give their fellow East Berliners a better life above protecting their own. The guards don't even know this is going on, so we have gotten all of the details from the secret radio station, which included getting special identity passes.

This one-way train to freedom is exactly where we are headed as we step off of the train and into another station, though tracking down a secretive train has been difficult. While I carefully watch my step out of the train, Mother's eyes roam the station in search of our next ride. She has to carefully scroll through the descriptions given on the radio to match them to our special train.

"There it is!" She bends slightly to alert me with a breathy voice.

To find which train she is talking about, all I have to do is follow the trail of smoke from my mother's pupils to the train that she has created from staring so passionately at it.

It looks just like any other train. Not suspicious at all. It just sits there waiting for its passengers to board like every other train, but it is not every other train. Seeing the people standing by it in the distance makes my stomach get caught somewhere between my lungs, and suddenly, nerves make it hard to breathe. Mother and I are so close. *All* of those people are so close. Everything in me wants to talk to them, hear what their plans were, and celebrate our journey to freedom, but common sense muffles my zeal. Even once we are on the train, I won't dare say anything. We are so close. I do not want to ruin it.

"Stop!"

A small band of East German patrol soldiers rush toward us through the station like loitering rats with a newfound purpose. Mother freezes and stares blankly.

So close.

"You're going to have to come with us," the largest rat demands, eyeing the bound down comforter shoved under Mother's arm.

Parched for words again, this time by another culprit, Mother mouths, "Stay here and wait," articulately. More than I can read her lips though, I can read her face.

As they take her away, I cannot help but cry.

Stupid down comforter.

Why did she have to bring it? I know that we are poor and would not have been able to afford another one, but it's not worth it! It did keep us warm while we were in the camp for a week, but I would rather be cold than lose my mother.

The winter air is bitter and nearly freezes my tears as I stand frozen in the middle of this bustling station. Here I am in the largest city in Germany, but I am completely alone. What if she doesn't come out? Will they come back for me? I may have sat in as Tante Lieschen taught her the routes, but none of it stuck and I can't seem to get a hold of it while everything else seems to be slipping away. I don't know where I will go or how to get to my relatives in West Berlin even if I did take the train.

Clutching the bag under my arm so hard that I might rip through, I begin to pray. No other plan I try to concoct on my own will be good enough. I just stand in the middle of the station forcing the passing people to maneuver around me, but no matter what, I am not moving from this spot until my mother comes back.

*   *   *

It seems like hours have passed by and so have many people, but I have not left my spot.

From the corner of my eye, I catch the rats scurrying out from where they last ran off to, and trailing closely behind them is my mother! Finally free to leave my post, I run to her, and she is able to break through the pack and do the same. As we close the gap between each other, I can clearly make out glistening tears being released from the corners of her eyes, and I imagine that she can see the same water show on me.

I think this is the first time that my tears have ever been wet with joy and not hurt.

The gap between us completely diminished, our bodies collide.

"Are you okay?" I manage to calm my heavy breathing to ask, "What did they do?"

Looking to see who's around, but seemingly not too concerned about who overhears she fills the past couple of hours in for me, "It was very scary, Siddi. They took me to a small, simple room, and there they interrogated, stripped, and searched me," her gaze wanders and her voice lowers with embarrassment when mentioning some of the details, "Nothing they found on me was incriminating . . . except the down comforter."

For a moment she pauses and takes a deep, loaded breath as if contemplating her decision to bring the suspicious item along, and I inhale and do the same.

"They started to make arrangements to have me transported somewhere that they wouldn't tell me . . ."

Hearing her describe what happened brings the scene vividly to life in my head, and seeing my mother having to face the possibility of being deported makes my legs weak even now that she is safe and in front of me.

"Luckily, a kind man came into the room at that point and intervened. He let me go, but only if I left the down comforter. I easily did!"

"I was so scared," I lie a little to her . . . I'm still scared.

Taking hold of my hand, she is quickly back to business. "We must go!"

Looking through the blur of people, I can see the underground train sitting in its usual spot just waiting for freedom-seeking passengers. Hand-in-hand, we run from the place where I have been stuck for what seems like forever to our final, fateful outlet.

I don't even want to look back.

ARRIVING IN NEUSTADT

Even the sparrow has found a home.

"We are so happy for you and your daughter," my Mother's cousin says as she pats her shoulder.

"Well we never could have done it without you," Mother replies with true sincerity welled in her voice, "Thank you so much for everything."

All of our belongings that we dropped off here for the past month had been gathered and packed for us by the family. Yesterday's events of Mother almost being transported and we permanently arriving into freedom all in the same day really wore us out, so we spent the night with my mother's relatives as planned. We could not have been more elated to see them, and they made our first night of freedom memorable with a delicious array of foods.

After about the third round of brief hugs and goodbyes, Mother and I grab our purses, and board the plane with the tickets to Frankfurt Main that my father had sent us. Though I am so happy to be going to a home that will be our own where I will have different clothes to wear everyday besides the same rags, I cannot help but feel like something is missing. It feels wrong to be leaving Jörg, but he is engaged to a girl named Ursula and plans to escape once they are married. I hope they hurry.

Finding our seats on the plane without the stress of looking suspicious and not being searched every step of the way feels so liberating. We make ourselves comfortable, and Mother is able to tell me our plans openly without fear in a normal tone of voice.

"Once the plane lands in Frankfurt Main, we have a train ride that will take a couple of hours, and then we will be in Neustadt, our new home." She holds her breath after that last word and looks toward the aisle. She turns her head back toward me as if she found what she was looking for and finishes, "Your father will be waiting there for us."

Still staring at me, I think she is waiting for my reaction, but I don't give her one. I just brush it off and put it out of my mind for now. I want to enjoy this time with my mother and revel in our accomplishment.

Finally being in a free world, a tremendous burden has been lifted off of our shoulders. I feel joyful and at peace. No more secrecy or not being able to trust people. Now I can eat bananas, chocolate, cake, and all of the delicious foods that I have never tasted! The people surrounding me every day are happier, and why wouldn't they be? They are free.

*   *   *

Only the shrill screech of the train coming to a stop could wake me out of my deep slumber.

"Are we here?" I ask in a groggy voice.

"Yes, get your bag."

I get my purse and scramble trying to make myself look alive. We get off of the train in the routine fashion that we have become so accustomed to, and as soon as we are off, Mother's neck grows a couple of centimeters so she can try to peer over the crowd. After a minute or two of searching, it retracts.

"This way."

She must have found my father. I am excited to live in free Germany, but I am not at all eager to see the man who abandoned us. I don't want him here acting like he did us a favor. Mother made all of this happen for me and her, not him.

"You made it," is his first comment to us, completely lacking enthusiasm.

There is no hugging, kissing, or any welcoming gestures.

"Yes, we did," Mother says trying to smile a little, but I detect some satisfaction of "we got you" in her grin.

With a stern nod, he turns while informing, "I got us a taxi."

Mother and I have to scurry to follow him as he is already trying to establish his authority over us.

In between brisk strides and heavy breaths I ask Mother, "Where are we going?"

"To our new home," she answers trying to excite me, "He has an apartment."

Not knowing how to respond or feel, I just look down at the ground. I am glad to have a new home, but I do not want to be stuck with my father in it. How can the three of us live together after everything that has happened?

Mother and I pack our suitcases into the taxi as my father stands by watching as if propping against the door is helpful. We all load into the vehicle, awkwardly squeezed together. I take the position that I plan to hold for the ride by laying my hands in my lap, leaning away from the center of the car, and staring out the window. No particular words or things that I should say or even want to say can come to mind. Most thoughts are too harsh to say to start our "new beginning", so I secretly vow to myself to stay silent… at least until we get to the apartment.

SURPRISE

The Lord sets prisoners free.

What seemed like the world's longest taxi ride finally is over. The car pulls up in front of a dingy brown apartment with an upside-down door lamp whose screws have swiveled loose. I am still grateful to have a place to live, but I must admit that I expected something nicer. I thought it would be more like the nice house we lived in before the war, but this apartment looks more like a bedraggled war survivor.

Mother and I lug our suitcases to the paint-chipped door that my father opens for us. Immediately upon entering through the door, we are standing in a bedroom. Despite the unorthodox layout of the apartment, I am curious to see the rest, and we continue through a small, narrow passage connecting to the next room that is almost too short to call a hallway. Oddly, my father doesn't udder a word or offer a complimentary tour of our new home. But once in the living room, I understand why.

I cannot believe this.

Sitting cozily in the living room is Erika, her husband, and her two children.

Steam is coming off of my mother. The fury she is about to unleash is undeniable. As if too stupid or oblivious to understand how messed up this situation is, the mistress and her family just stare at us newcomers indifferently. There are no signs of any mental activity from Erika or her husband. I have never seen anyone like them.

To make up for their inactivity, Mother begins to overcompensate, beating into my father with dagger words and twice-betrayed jabs. He yells back at her, and suddenly I am in our little room on the farm again. As they continue to battle, Erika's husband sits back a little more comfortably on the couch and mechanically brings his cigarette to his mouth and pulls it away with a cloud of smoke while he intensely watches the corner fight he put money on. If he is even capable of feeling, I think he is enjoying himself.

Finally the screaming subsides with a, "You're disgusting," thrown by my mother, and she storms over to me.

Shaking in disbelief that my father has wronged us once again but even worse than I thought he was capable of, I dig my head into her shoulder.

"I do not want to live here," I say with a quivering voice, but then the meek emotion that was in me disappears. Only anger is left, and I lift my head and repeat looking straight at my father, "I do not want to live here."

He stares back with his hands hanging limp at his sides looking even more stupid than the adulteress' family.

With that, Mother pulls me into the front bedroom.

A plethora of upset words pour out of her all at once, "I'm so sorry, Siddi . . . . How could he? . . . After two years . . . How dare he . . . I've worked so hard . . . They do nothing . . . I don't know . . ."

Her knees buckle beneath her, and her bottom meets the floor. I squat down next to her trying to keep it together as her tears flow. With each word that escapes from her mouth, she gets a little lighter and calmer.

Restricting the flow of anymore tears, she wipes her salty, soaked cheeks revealing that determined look that I know so well and says, "I am sorry. We are free, Sigrid, and we should be thankful."

I nod my head because I am thankful, but I feel guilty for wanting to run all the way back to Tante Lieschen's apartment in not free East Berlin.

"I know this is not right to live like this, but we must for now. We have nowhere else to go."

"I know; we're stuck," I interject with a bitterly sarcastic chuckle.

Trying to ease me, she keeps going, "Yes, but we will get through this like we have with everything else. Just keep praying and have faith."

Silently I pray to God the same prayer I used to pray on the haystacks, "Lord, take me far from here."

I will carry on with my life. I am not sure what tomorrow brings, but God will provide like he has before. We survived a war and escaped to freedom, and even though my father has hurt my mother and me so badly by forcing us under the same roof as his mistress' family, I still have hope.

I know that I will get out of here someday because *I am free.*

Afterword

Finally at twelve years old, I was free, but I still had many struggles to face in the free world. My mother and I were so thankful for everyone who helped us in our great escape, especially Tante Lieschen.

Little did we know the day we left East Germany for good that it would be the last time we would ever see Mother's older sister. Their only communication was by mail, and Mother continued to send her packages and money. In order to survive in East Berlin, Tante Lieschen became an underground peddler selling food and cigarettes that my mother would send her on the black market. She lived a dangerous life but she was very clever and never got caught. When we received the news that she passed, Mother and I were devastated that we could not attend her funeral since we had escaped illegally, but Tante Lieschen was a wonderful Christian lady who got to go be with the Lord.

Five months after we arrived in Neustadt, out of fear of losing his prestigious job, my father got the three of us a different apartment to live in without Erika's family. Shortly after we moved, Erika and her family were transported by the West German government back to East Germany for stealing. Since they lost their meal ticket, my dad, they survived for awhile by stealing from various shops. The East German government gladly took them back because they were wanted there for crimes they had committed before escaping. It was big news in the newspapers and everywhere. Mother was happy they were gone, but my dad had a new steady love by that time: the bottle.

The apartment we moved to was above a corner Gasthaus on a very narrow, stone street. There was a walk-in pantry. My parents placed a small bed in there and it became my room. That was where I spent most of my private time among the groceries and stored items, but it was never a bedroom to me. Just a pantry. My mother and father spent most of their free time downstairs in the Gasthaus, but I only rarely joined them for a meal. I had no interest in being there and watching my alcoholic father get drunk.

With everything my father kept putting us through, I would ask my mother why she was staying with him. When she finally answered me, I was surprised by her answer. Mother had a long term plan, which might sound selfish to some, but I eventually understood when I left home and got married. She knew that my father's work had a generous benefit package, which included medical and life insurance. She decided that she was still legally married to my dad and she would not give up what she deserved after all she had gone through during and after the war. She had helped my father to recover after the war, and she had practically raised their two children alone.

Me in the Norsee.

My first summer in Neustadt, I received an invitation from Aunt Charlotte and Cousin Maria to come and visit them on the island of Norderney located in the Nordsee. That was my first trip to take alone.

I had the greatest time of my life there. I was loved by both of them and was spoiled to the fullest. They had some idea of my childhood, and they gave me everything, which I was thankful for and gladly accepted. There, I celebrated my thirteenth birthday, and I never wanted to leave. But Mother wouldn't allow it, and I had to return to finish school.

135

Needless to say, I was behind in all subjects because I had missed many weeks of school for our getaway. I studied and worked hard to catch up, and after a time, I did. This time, I had teachers who cared about me and understood what I had gone through. They knew I was a refugee. I hated being known as 'the refugee', and I was afraid that it would define me for the rest of my life. However, the term disappeared after a while, and I became the East German girl. I made friends at school and very few kids looked down on me like they had in Tramstow.

I had one very special girlfriend, Gisela. (Gisela now lives outside of Milwaukee.) She and I clicked right away because she saw into my heart. I was thrilled to have a true girlfriend who I could be with, talk to, and go places together. I became like another daughter to her mother, and her father was very quiet and easygoing.

When my parents moved from the apartment above the Gasthaus to a new one in a complex for government employees, Gisela's family came to my rescue. As an employee, my father was given the option of an apartment with either one or two bedrooms, and he chose the one bedroom. He told me it wasn't his concern where I would live and that I needed to figure it out. So Gisela's family welcomed me to stay with them even though their apartment was already too small for their large family, and I squeezed in a bed with Gisela and her younger sister. I remember going to see my mom in the daytime and telling her that I had no place to stay, and I would plead for her to talk to her husband.

Mother taking care of her flowers at their new apartment.

She seemed to have no will of her own. She was a slave to my father, for at this time, my father's drinking was worse than ever. When she complained about it, it only fueled his fire. He started getting mean and calling her names and accusing her of things she never did. Several times he was physically abusive and would pin her against the wall and hit her. Sometimes, I would try to get between them, and my father would end up hitting me. Then in the mornings, he would act as if nothing happened.

Eventually, Gisela, her sister, and I couldn't continue sleeping together in a single bed, and my father finally allowed me to stay with them again. My father wouldn't let me sleep on the couch because it was new and he thought I would ruin it, but he pushed their two single beds together for us all to sleep on. Luckily, I wouldn't have to stay there long.

For a while, Mother and my father lived their lives, and I lived mine. I attended high school and graduated early. From there, I went to nursing school. I wanted to become a labor and delivery nurse, and my schooling involved working several hours a week in a private maternity clinic. More than actually wanting to work, I wanted to stay away from my father's apartment as much as possible.

Through my father's work, I met several GIs whom he would meet with after his office hours. On one occasion, he had my mother and me go to dinner with him to meet with an American soldier. Throughout the meal, I was embarrassed by my father's drunken state, but the soldier was nice and we had a pleasant conversation. I told him a little bit about my life that night, and apparently I left an impression on him because he told the assistant chaplain at the base about me and my home life.

When this Christian soldier heard about me, he felt that God wanted him to do something to take me out of that situation. I happened to be home with Mother one afternoon when the doorbell rang, and out in the hall stood three American soldiers, one of them was the assistant chaplain. He asked me if I wanted to come and live with him and his family. I said I did want to because I believed that this was God answering my prayers. So even though it was hard, I left my mother and nursing school and went with the soldier, Pastor Orr.

For about eight months I lived on the air base with Pastor Orr and his family. Even though they had three girls and one on the way, I still had my own room and was treated like part of the family. Communicating was a struggle since I knew very little English and their German was sparse, but we managed somehow. They taught me things, and I helped around the house and with the children.

Every Sunday and a few other days a week, we went to church on the air base together. Several young soldiers also attended, and after the service, they would come over to the Orr's for dinner. All of the soldiers would talk and have a good time, but they spoke too fast for me to understand or even be able to enter the conversation. Mostly I would take care of the baby and listen.

After a time, Pastor Orr and his wife told me that their friend, one of the Sunday dinner soldiers, was an electrician from Indiana. Then they shocked me and said that he might become my husband. I didn't believe it, and I remember laughing because the thought of actually leaving Germany seemed unreal and out of the question to me. I never thought that I would leave my motherland and marry an American GI. I did not know that this major event was part of God's plan for my life.

After heavy persuasion from the Orr's, I went on a motorcycle ride with this soldier, Jerry, and that was the beginning of our dating. We didn't have much time to date and get to know each other well because his time in Germany was coming to an end, but we got married quickly anyway because we believed that God had brought us together.

My husband, Jerry, in uniform.

Reluctantly, my father signed the papers to allow me to marry since I was under twenty-one. So at a young age, Jerry and I were married in front of a small group of American friends. My parents did not come, but they sent me a robe as a wedding gift.

Just a year later, our first child, a baby girl, was born in Germany. My husband's four years with the Air Force were up, so he reenlisted for another four years of service. He was supposed to report back to the States, but he asked for an extension to stay longer in Germany. The Air Force allowed him to stay for another six months. This extension helped us to have a little time to finalize the paperwork for me to get permission to enter the U.S. because it progressed very slowly since I escaped from East Germany and my brother still lived there.

When the papers at last came through, my mother came to Otterberg the day we were leaving for the Frankfurt airport. I said good-bye to her on a street in the little town where I had been living with my new husband and child. My father did not come with her to say his good-byes. We both cried and hugged and cried some more. She was glad that I would have a better life, but I felt nothing but sorrow for leaving her with her out-of-control, alcoholic husband.

When I left for America with Jerry, he told me that he couldn't promise that I would get to see my mother again, and it was ten years until I did. Soon after I left, my father finally went to a rehabilitation facility in the Black Forest, and he came back healed. I was so happy for my mother because she got to have a couple of really happy years with him. After all she had stood by him through, she got the happiness she deserved. Unfortunately, after two years of being alcohol-free, my father died of cirrhosis of the liver. Before he passed, he also wrote me a letter apologizing for everything he put me through and asked for me to forgive him, and I did. I wrote back telling him that I forgave him and that I loved him.

Jerry, my daughter, and I landed at McGuire Air Base in New Jersey, and from there we went by military bus to Penn Station where we took a train to Evansville, Indiana. There my husband's mother and sister greeted us. After spending a week with them, we went to Warren Air Force Base in Cheyenne, Wyoming, my husband's place of assignment.

Already I was having culture shock after seeing my first television and all of the different scenery, but my new life as a military wife would prove to be even more of a shock.

The cold weather, flat countryside, and cowboys didn't make me feel at home out there, and since Jerry worked at missile sites and his duty required schoolings and other secret things I never knew about, I was alone most of the time. But the only reason I did feel right at home was because of the camaraderie I had with the other military families. I felt accepted and safe even though I was miles from home, and I knew they would always be there for me.

A good example of other military people looking out for us happened when I was almost nine months pregnant. My husband and I were driving on a deserted country road with our daughter when a snowstorm struck and our car got stuck. Jerry followed a fence along the road to lead him back through the haze, and he returned with his friend, one of the military police. The MP had to carry me to his car, and he wouldn't stop making jokes about how heavy I was! Those were the kind of friends I made, and military life really showed me that I was a respected female, wife, and mother.

When we first got to Cheyenne, I knew almost no English, so much of my alone time when Jerry was gone was spent watching soap operas. I would try to understand what they were saying and learn the new sounds and words that comprise the language, and when my husband came home, I would ask him about the words of which I was unsure. He would tell me and correct my improper English until eventually, I became fluent. It was a struggle learning a foreign language on my own, but thanks to television and my husband, I learned English.

For years, our family hopped around the country wherever Jerry's assignment was, and over the course of those years, we had a total of three daughters. Finally, we settled in Terre Haute, IN. I went back to school and became a secretary at the local high school. I worked there for twenty years, and I must say I was proud of myself for going from knowing no English to holding a job that required me to type and talk to people all day in English.

When the girls were still in grade school, my mother came over and stayed with us for six months. I acted as the translator between my mother and my family, and we all had a great time. When the girls got older, two of my daughters, my husband, and I were able to go to Germany in 1981. We got to be with her on Christmas in Bremen where she had moved to be closer to her other family. After this trip, we got to go back several times, but this was the only trip that we would be able to see my brother.

When my mother and I escaped, Jörg said he would escape too once he got married to his fiancée, Ursula, but by that time, it was too late. People were being killed on the spot, and security was even tighter. So when we went to visit him, it was an experience to be back, especially to see the wall.

Visiting East Berlin was difficult, and since East Germans were not allowed to leave for any reason, we had to get special passes to enter. Even though Jörg's family did not live in East Berlin, that was where we met. Before my family and I could cross over, each one of us was interrogated and searched. Jörg and his family stood just steps away on the other side waiting, and finally, after over twenty years, we were reunited. We hugged and kissed, and we were so elated to see each other.

They took us to a restaurant where we ate and talked and talked. I could not keep my eyes off my handsome brother. I was so proud of the man he had become. We loved each other so much, and there is nothing comparable to being with your own, loving blood.

After eating, my daughters wanted to walk around the city. In their classes at home, they had been learning about Communism and the wall, and they were fascinated to be in the heart of it. Just walking the streets, I was scared, but I never told anybody. For some reason, I felt like the prowling soldiers with their familiar, scary boots would know that I had run away many years ago and they would force me to stay. Even though I had fears, my younger daughter had none. Taking pictures was 'Verboten', but she wanted to take some anyway. My brother was so nervous and kept begging her to stop because he could get in big trouble. However, when we got home, they ended up being neat souvenirs to have.

After we did a little sight-seeing, we went to visit my uncle, Bruno, who lived in East Berlin. Getting to his apartment was difficult though. We had to split into three smaller groups (large groups were considered suspicious), and my husband and daughters were not to speak so that no one would know they were Americans. Once we got into the apartment, Bruno hung a thick blanket on the door so that nobody could hear us. We sat around his table and had a great time, and he talked about life in East Berlin and how he hated every minute of it.

By midnight, we had to be out of East Germany, so Jörg took us to the border. We had an incident where my husband got separated from us through all of the searches, but once we found out he had been forced to already board the train, I jumped for joy, turned around and saw my brother waving on the other side, and got on the train. Little did I know that would be the last time that I would ever see him.

Jörg passed away at fifty years of age after many months in a hospital. Mom went to visit him several times, but she could never find out what illness he had. The doctor could never diagnose his sickness, for medical facilities were still very primitive in East Germany. Doctors came to the conclusion that Jörg didn't get the proper nourishment when he was growing up and his body finally gave out.

My mother and I stayed in contact through letters and frequent phone calls, and after that first visit, I got to see her every four years. She was very funny and pleasant in her older years. She always made me laugh with her old, funny German sayings. At the age of 95, my mother passed away in her sleep. She was and is my inspiration, and I am grateful that after her hectic life, the Lord took her away so peacefully.

Because of her, I was able to be free. Seeing my brother stuck in Communism (which I didn't even know that word until I got to the U.S. because those negative terms were not allowed) absolutely broke my heart. I was thankful before, but going back to East Berlin made me realize just how blessed I am. God had woven certain people and experiences into my life for a reason. If it weren't for every series of events that occurred, I would not be free in America with the loving family I have today. In life, there are people whose help I could never forget and there are people that I have to forgive, but I will always be thankful for every blessing and never forget who I am . . . the East German Girl.

Glossary

Deutsch Demokratische Republik—German Democratic Republic

Frau—Mrs.

Fröliche Weihnachten O Tannenbaum—Merry Christmas Oh Christmas Tree

Gasthaus—bar/restaurant

GI—government issue; personnel

Herr—Mr.

MP—military police

Mutti—mommy

Nordsee—North Sea

Opa—grandfather

Tante—aunt

U-Bahn—subway

Verboten—forbidden

Author Biography

Because of my life circumstances and experiences, I endured many hardships (as do many of us). But with the knowledge and strength I acquired from conquering every obstacle, I have chosen to put them into words and share my story to inspire others. Although I am an East German Girl, I now reside with my husband and dear family in the Midwest.